Poems Given of God to the Heart Reach

...Simply Because They Teach.

EVELYN A. JOSEPH

Sources used in the preparation of this book include: Google.com, *The Oxford Language Dictionary, The Merriam-Webster Dictionary, The Cambridge Dictionary,* vocabulary.com, RhymeZone.com, thesaurus.com, as well as *The Hebrew-Greek Keyword Study Bible.*

All Scripture passages are taken from the King James Version of the Bible. Public domain.

Poems Given of God, To the Heart Reach
Simply Because They Teach
Copyright © 2024 by Evelyn Joseph
ISBN: 978-1-685730-70-3

Published by Word and Spirit Publishing
P.O. Box 701403
Tulsa, Oklahoma 74170
wordandspiritpublishing.com

Printed in the United States of America. All rights reserved under International Copyright Law. Content and/or cover may not be reproduced in whole or in part in any form without the expressed written consent of the Publisher.

DEDICATION

No one deserves this honor except you, my love. Marcel Joseph, your knowledge and achievements of past years have anchored me in a way I could never have imagined. As I followed through to the finalization of this assignment, I realized early into the project that I was doing and saying things that did not reflect me, but indeed, reflected you. People often say, "A man and his wife after so many years start looking like brother and sister." I'm of the thought that we not only look alike, but we sound, act, and believe alike. This work was, indeed, written by the two of us, because God used your "up-scaled" form of speech through me—much of which I never would have thought I had retained. Ninety percent of what we will expose the Body of Christ to was derived from our teachings, from the two of us. For your sacrifice, I thank you much and love you more.

CONTENTS

Acknowledgments viii
Foreword by Marcel Joseph ix
Preface x
1   Jesus, My Judge 1
2   Wells of Springing Water 3
3   Overriding the Enemy 4
4   Calamity 5
5   My Peace 6
6   Conferring Superiority 7
7   The Word 9
8   Room for You 11
9   Arise 12
10   Yes, He Did 13
11   Our Schedule 15
12   Get on with the Show 16
13   Humanity 18
14   I Come 20
15   Who He Made Me to Be 21
16   Approach 22
17   Control of Soul 23
18   Our Fellowship 24
19   God's Way 26
20   Psalm 43 27
21   Finish Your Course 29
22   Rejoicing 31
23   Know His Voice 32
24   When Jesus Called 34
25   Happy Are We 35
26   Bright, Shining Light 36
27   Commonsense Nonsense 37
28   Ancient of Days 38

29	He Found Me	41
30	Closer, Much Closer	42
31	Children of Light	43
32	Watch and Pray	44
33	That Kind of Word	45
34	Mrs. Rose Mitchell	46
35	Looking Back	48
36	Rock of Ages	50
37	Victory	51
38	Without You	52
39	In His Image	54
40	Privileged Bunch	57
41	Run, Walk, Talk	59
42	The World Has Set You F-r-e-e	61
43	You're the Apple of God's Own Eye	64
44	More Than Gold	67
45	Good and Upright Are You	69
46	Seedling	70
47	I Give Thanks to You	71
48	He Brought Me Through	73
49	Joy and Glory	75
50	I've Got a Promise	77
51	My Echo	80
52	He Washed Us White as Snow	81
53	Be Aware	84
54	Dig It—Dung It	87
55	You Three Have Entered In	89
56	We Must (Retain)	91
57	He Said, He Saw	97
58	He Did, He Did It, He Died	99
59	Damsel, Arise	100
60	How Can It Be?	101
61	I'll Speak for You	102

62	The Ingredient	104
63	It Will Be Well	107
64	Recouped It All	109
65	Good Morning, Jesus	112
66	Cities of Unrest	116
67	Of Which We Are	119
68	O Isles	120
69	Political Atmosphere	122
70	We Bow to the Bid	124
71	Oh, How I've Changed	126
72	Spirit of All Ages	129
73	I Must Chant	133
74	Finding Grace	134
75	Innocent Blood	135
76	Trees of the Field	136
77	Wield the Word	138
78	Battle	139
79	Speak His Name	140
80	Reservoir for My Ministry	142
81	The Worth of What Is Missing	145
82	Solid Rock	147
83	Sing from the Heart	149
84	I Vow	152
85	We Win	154
86	To Do Your Will	156
87	We Thank You	158
88	Your Now Is Yours	160
89	Flows My Portion	163
90	You Aren't Wearing That	166
91	Conversion from Perversion	168
92	The Highway of the Upright	170
93	One Mountain	172
94	I Look	173

95	The Vault of Heaven	174
96	Commanded Blessing	175
97	Send Him On	176
98	I Have the Remedy	179
99	Lift Up Your Eyes and Look	181
100	How Would You Be Rated?	183
101	Every Way	185
102	Credibility	188
103	At Last	190
104	Thoughts	192
105	Copacetic	194
106	The Fast	196
107	Abler	201
108	Hunch	203
109	Possession	205
110	We Come	207
111	Forgive Me	209
112	Aging	213
113	Holy Matrimony	215
114	Prosperity	217
115	My Place in Battle	218
116	Tirhza	219
117	Great Grace	221
118	Ya Gotta Wanna	222
119	I Am	223
120	Perspective	225
121	Oh, Magnify the Lord with Me	227
122	Here's a Reverberating Sound	229
123	You Mold Our Hearts	232
124	Come with Thanksgiving	233
125	The Greatest Sound I've Ever Heard	235
126	Catacombs (Cris Joseph)	237

ACKNOWLEDGMENTS

We at Sword and Psalm Ministry, aka Joseph Ministries, have had a mandate from God—for almost thirty-nine years now—"to increase the Christian expression in the life of every believer with whom we come in contact." We do this in different ways, whether through teaching, preaching, or ministering through song. We have been blessed to have been chosen by God to fulfill this awesome request. That is exactly what it was. God did not tell us what to do; He politely asked, "Will you preach My Gospel?" And we responded with the words, "Yes, Lord, we will preach Your Gospel." That has continued even until today.

However, we are not on this trek alone. Throughout the years, whatever help we needed was provided. So it was with this project.

Andy Sheets was the first to put his hands to my scribbles, and believe you me, that is the proper description of my handwriting! Despite that, Andy, you were able to do a significant piece of work in a timely fashion. Great job, Andy.

Tirhza Louis, as busy as you always are, I marvel at your willingness not to be selfish with your time and abilities. All the back-and-forth with the editing and the never-ending correcting of all my blunders—mainly due to my shying away from technology—would have discouraged the best of them. Not you. Just sticking with me proves the depth of your stability. Much appreciation and love for your time and expertise!

—Evelyn Joseph

FOREWORD

There are times in life when you observe things that are done that are inspiring and masterfully constructed in such a way as to leave you in utter appreciation of the work. Yet when one considers the source, nothing less is to be expected of them, in that this is the norm and coincides with their method of operation. Well, such is not the case in this situation—although the work in which you're about to take part was certainly masterfully put together, one would not have expected it of the author. I can say that for I have known her for fifty-seven years and have observed all of her skill sets, one of which pointed to the creation of this poetic masterpiece.

On the other hand, when I considered the Source behind these words, I realize the Author is none other than the Spirit of God using a yielded vessel to communicate these wonderful rhythmic lines meant to lodge in the heart of man—undeniable principles that convey the truth in a harmonic flow that pierces the heart.

The timing, rhythm, and cadence of these embedded biblical principles find their way into the very spirit of the reader, bringing to life an unforgettable episode that one can go back to, identify with, and experience the relevance of over and over again.

I am convinced that the reading of this work will have a lasting effect on how one sees things in the future concerning anything from relationships to the contemporary issues we all deal with daily.

One will encounter stunning ebbs and flows from shocking to subtle paces, which at some points will jolt the reader and at other times gently lay out a truth that will almost sneak up on the reader and reveal the power of that truth smoothly.

Moreover, the introduction of each theme seems to beckon the reader to look ahead to the end of the poem with some degree of knowing, to some degree, how it will end. Such is futile in this regard, as the anticipated culmination rarely aligns with any preconceived ideas the reader may conjure up. Enjoy.

PREFACE

The COVID-19 pandemic provided Marcel and me with days, weeks, even months of waking up in the mornings in our own bed.

That alone was quite different for us. However, I will say that God blessed me each morning in how He chose to awaken me during these months. It all started just days after the shutdown, between the early morning hours of 3:00 to 5:00 a.m.

It began with me hearing a single word. In saying "word," understand that I am not speaking of the Scriptures. No, just a single word was what I was hearing in the beginning.

Also, it was obvious to me that activity had been going on for some time, although I was asleep.

After coming to a consciousness of what I had been doing, somehow I knew to carry on with that activity. And soon after, I was sensing another word, then another, until there was a full-fledged sentence.

Now, that was always the point at which I needed to remove myself from bed, for several different reasons.

First, I needed to document what was said, and I knew there was more to come. My need and desire were to get alone with God. That pursuit always developed into a comparable poem.

That last statement is reason enough for me to be convinced God is involved in all of this. I say that because I have never been favorable toward poetry. I had always thought of them as childish. The effort it took to speak or write a word with the intent of matching it up with another word of like sound? I perceived that to be quite foolish, whether it be comedy or classic.

But God has chosen the foolish things of the world to confound the wise, and He has chosen the weak things of the world to confound the things that are mighty. (1 Corinthians 1:27) Nothing was more foolish than my thoughts on poems. Oh, of late, of course, however, that has certainly changed.

And why not? After all, there are many, many more poems to come.

1

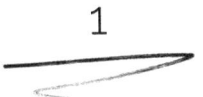

Jesus, My Judge

Composed February 15, 2024

As we have been taught to strive with words,
we send forth our legal cause, nothing deferred.
Forensics agree, my right to be free.
That is my cause, my cause, my plea.
Jesus, the Judge, did rescue me.
My Defender, my Pleader to the enemy
and adversary,
a valid legal case against him will be.
God will indict, the world will see.
As we were taught, we strive with words.
That legal comment, sufficient for the pause.
As it was most certainly the proven cause.

This is my case, my plea,
Jesus, my Judge, did rescue me.
Forensics agree,
check the grave, He is not there, for
He is now in me, and that secures my right to be free.
My Defender, my Pleader,
now has a valid legal case against him,
the enemy, who is the adversary.
All infractions cannot be tallied,
but as the shadow of death was, at all costs, valleyed,
I proclaim our God will most surely indict,
thereby putting all things right.

Using only one illegal action, only one.
That being the crucifixion of His Son.

A judicial and forensic cause that cannot,
will not, be forgiven, not ever.
No litigation or plea from the adversary
will ever cancel his punishment throughout eternity.
Adjudicator again, he will never be, and that
now shall be his perplexity.
No out-of-court settlement decree.
Eternally lost he will be,
The CEO of hell, you see.

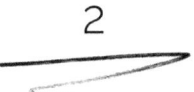

Wells of Springing Water

Sow in the land where you are,
God will bless you by far.
You will wax great and increase,
having much more to release.
Possessions will enable you to give more and more,
from that bounty of a great store.
God is blessing you for what you do.
Some who know you,
will envy you too.
You cannot help that; this is a given fact.
You've found wells of springing water,
make no apologies for that.

His paydays will always arrive.
And that you must realize
There is a well of springing water released to me.
That I promise, you will see.
If you don't believe it now, you soon will,
when you see it in my till,
and it will be there in my written will.

3

Overriding the Enemy

He came in, then I woke up,
soon after that, then filled my cup.
Though out of the realm of my understanding,
peace to me was His granting.
Then out of nowhere,
that light I did see.
He imparted that affordability.
I know now more,
than I ever have before.
He did it, I couldn't.
I never relented, I wouldn't.
He prevented what I could not see,
overriding the enemy.
All because He loves me.

4

Calamity

Oh, that my grief was thoroughly weighed.
My calamity in the balance together laid.
Heavier than the sand of the sea, I perceive.
The arrows of the Almighty are not within me.
I will charge not my God with this calamity.
The poisons that wreck my body, you see,
are not the terrors of God in array against me.
There is no taste in the white of an egg, no doubt,
but the yellow within will help balance it out.
As salt is the default for the white of an egg,
God is within for every pain, sickness, and plague.
I am not made to possess vanity.
Worrisome nights are not appointed to me.
I will arise when the night is gone.
There will be no tossing to and from till dawn.
There is no anguish of my spirit;
if I complain, my soul does fear it.

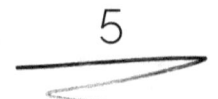

My Peace

I'll say my peace and be brief.
Time is running out.
The lies built by the devil prove no guilt, but doubt.
Know your right to be free from his encumbrances,
that evil god of redundancies.
I tell you what I am saying is on cue.
The devil won't push the button and come on through.
He won't accost you.
He knows he is no match for your assigned angels,
so he tucks his tail in retreat.
He wouldn't volunteer to evacuate,
until you used your voice to eradicate.
Him you never need to tolerate.
Make the decision; it's never too late.
How great.
Your vessel will never belong to him again, Amen!

Conferring Superiority

Thank You, Lord, for Your word.
The most melodic sound I've ever heard.
An instrumental
only will never be,
as calming as Your song pursuing me.

He sings and will sing His words to me,
a special feature and quality,
conferring superiority; it is my God's property.
He sings and will sing His words to me.

His words make the song what it is meant to be,
a calming collection of thoughts reviving me.
The moans and groans within any song
occasionally seem a bit too long.
The oohs and aahs express strong emotions,
but they fall short of the word's notions.

He sings and will sing His words to me,
a special feature and quality,
conferring superiority;
it is my God's property.
He sings and will sing His words to me.

His words give a belief,
and sometimes opinions,
with a mental image or explanations.
It is so distinct what the Word can do,
at all times
comforting too.
And it will distinguish
the good from the bad,
the right from the wrong,
the sad from the glad;
setting always apart
the characteristics of the heart;
marked by excellence, easily perceived,
and very likely achieved.
When you believe, then you receive.

He sings and will sing His words to me,
a special feature, and quality
conferring superiority;
it is my God's property.
He sings and will sing His words to me.

The Word

We are the flock You feed,
every day, for every need.
Dear Lord, we sit at Your table on this day.
Our spirits skip like rams and lambs,
for what You have to say.
Not as the mountains in display of dismay,
but with joy we replay Your stay.
That is our identifiable character.
It's who we are,
it's who we are.
So, as I mull over and cull over Your Word,
nothing there, my Lord, to reject.
That which applies to me I accept.
The Word that sealed me,
healed me, delivered me, set me free;
the Word that construct and instructs,
clued me when it renewed me,
giving me guiding information.
I can now see, for it set me free.
My witness is in heaven.
My record on high.
My help comes from the Word, I cannot deny.
If you have ears to hear, you'd best hear what I say.
The Word of God will provide a bit more,
than sustenance each day.

For in the afterlife, that's all time to come,
we are promised a stay with the Spirit,
the Father, and His dear Son.
Receive the seed of the Word into good ground.
Hear it, understand it, bear fruit
that's the truth.
A hundred-, sixty-, thirty-fold,
the Word grows.
And helps you to be bold.

8

Room for You

God has made a venue of view for you,
anointed with a corporate voice too.
You will be there,
because you care,
and it is your time to share.
As there is always room
for another piece of lace
in an overstuffed suitcase.
There is also room in the vineyard for you,
never too many
in any one city.
But should you be missing,
what a pity.

Arise

*T*he mighty God of Israel to you says, "Arise!
"Go where you are led to go."
The mighty God of Israel to you says, "Arise!
"Do what you were called to do."
He is with you.
You will not go alone,
never, ever alone.
Listen, believe,
trust, honor,
obey, receive.
The mighty God of Israel to you says, "Arise!
"Arise in your distress."
He will answer.
Hearing you is what He does,
and believe you me, that He loves.
Your comfort is His to give, and that He'll always relive.
His terror will protect for it is your default.
Never override that thought.
None will pursue and overtake you.
You will not be alone.
Listen, believe,
trust, honor,
obey, receive.
The mighty God of Israel to you says, "Arise!"

10

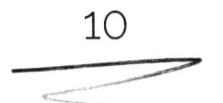

Yes, He Did

He was led as a sheep to the slaughter.
Like a lamb dumb before His shearer.
So opened He not His mouth.
No, opened He not His mouth.
Jesus, the Son of the Father,
the only Son, if only you believe.
So He did; yes, He did.
For us all, that He did.
He did for you,
when He did for all.
So, for us all, that He did.
Yes, He did.

Great humiliation, that vile in us all, void in Him,
for His body was not a sinful one,
like in humanity, and I mean all of them.
But His judgment was a separation,
from none other than God, my Father.
Who shall declare His generation,
without reservation?
His life was taken from earth in that space of time,
oh my.
The prophet who spoke these words
spoke not of another.
Indulge me while I preach to you as a mother.
Jesus, the only One who can save!

If you believe with your heart
before you depart,
you, too, can be saved, set apart,
delivered from sin, sickness, and poverty.
Just believe Jesus is the Son of God,
I plea.
He went to the cross, died in your place to set you free,
three days in the grave, and then He arose,
for the freedom of all, I am told,
for their liberty from that penalty.
That He did for you and for me.

11

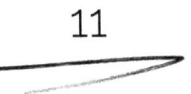

Our Schedule

A portion of our daily routine should always be scheduled:
morning, evening, night.
Any time of the twenty-four-hour day is right.
Sit alone with Him and meditate.
If out of sync, you are still not late.
When you sense it is time for prayer,
never hesitate to go right there.
The Word you have in you will speak to God for you.
Sensing you have come to the prayer's end,
pick up the Bible that's your friend.
Now, entering in, you'll see something new.
It's time to explore that certain word
you have read before,
giving you good insight into the context of that Scripture,
a clearer picture,
helping you understand more than what the ear heard
of that Word.

12

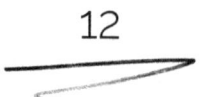

Get On with the Show

Stand down, jump back.
Whatever lingo you know.
Only the Holy Ghost will rule this show.
It's a show of power and not defeat.
A show of commitment and not retreat.
The Bible tells you,
well, you know, every now and then,
you've got to let go.
Get on with the show.
Extend your hand, obey the command.
The devil's saying what God just said, don't do.
Take out your checkbook and do it twice.
That blow to his head would be so nice.
Do it right.

Stand down, jump back.
Whatever lingo you know.
Only the Holy Ghost will rule this show.
It's a show of power and not defeat.
A show of commitment and not retreat.
The enemy has nothing to do with this issue.
Out of his eyes, the water will flow, pass him the tissue.

Get all excited, it's time to cheer.
The time to spring to the church, is most certainly here.
If you allow a virus to interrupt your stride.

It's now time to get out, there is no longer reason to hide.
Get all excited about the greet-and-meet
that comes after "stand to your feet."
Then it's time to worship and praise.
You've certainly missed that in the past days.
For some that grew to a year or two.
Don't turn around now if I'm talking about you.
If in all that time, you didn't give a dime,
it's time to respect that God of mine.

Get all excited, it's time to cheer!
The spring to the church is almost here.
Now, in my church the next to be done
is to preach and teach His Kingdom come.
But if your doctrine is not right,
there you are,
listening for something you think is wrong,
not even able to hum along,
with the song.

Issues of the heart, sometimes not, right?
will most certainly skew your sight.
Release your concerns to the Trinity.
You will be cared for throughout infinity.

Stand down, jump back.
Whatever lingo you know.
Only the Holy Ghost will rule this show.
It's a show of power and not defeat.
A show of commitment, not retreat.

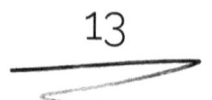

Humanity

*Y*ou may not agree, but it seems to me,
there is far more sympathy,
for animals than humanity.
Watch the commercials on TV.
They always seem to hype it up,
Saying, "Let's save the life of that pup.
"Go help that fawn trapped in that pond."
A homeless cat they see as an
embarrassment to all of mankind,
and that's fine.
But how is it, out of the same,
mouth will flow "abort that fetus"?
When we stand up to support the innocent,
then they want to beat us.
Somehow we have it in reverse.
Go to the Word, let's rehearse.
Genesis one and twenty-six:
what we have dominion over
is there in the mix.
Fish of the sea, simple to me.
Fowl of the air, everywhere.
Cattle and every mammal that creeps.
God gave to us that release.
But the nature of the issue has flipped.

Many think we have the right of
dominion over little people.
I will say, they don't see them that way.
And I have heard some say,
"It's just a googly-eyed glob.
"Try to give it life,
"and we will raise up a mob."
"Don't infringe upon my liberty,"
is what they say.
Well, the only rights
in that whole scenario
should have been granted
to the fetus, you know.
Rights from God to breathe
and be pleased.
Why endanger your eternity
by marring your integrity?
There is a family who wants that "live" tissue,
and that is the issue.

14

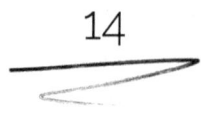

I Come

I waited patiently for the Lord.
He inclined unto me and heard.
He heard my every word.
He brought me up out of that horrible pit,
to where, I now sit,
here in fellowship with His flock,
and with my feet on the rock.
There is now a new song in my mouth.
It's about praise, my voice to raise.
God is about praise.
Many will see and fear,
and trust in the Lord so dear.
Blessed is the one who makes Him his trust.
He respects not the proud,
who lie and are filled with lust.
Sacrifice and offering He did not desire.
Burnt offerings, sin offerings, He did not require.
So, I say, I, I come.
Come.
In the volume of the book,
much is written of me.
Somehow I know it is filled with victory.
Your love is written within my heart.
I delight to do Your will, my God.
I am delighted to do my part.

15

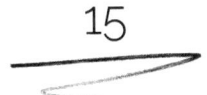

Who He Made Me to Be

The Word says I'm a king and priest
unto my God.
That's who He made me to be.
That throne, being established in righteousness,
makes it an abomination to commit wickedness.
The Word says I am a king and priest
unto my God.
That's who He made me to be.
But the wrath of a king is as messengers of death.
However, the wise, will pacify no less,
I guess.

16

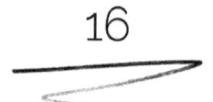

Approach

*I*n strict obedience to Your
detailed instructions, I come.
All persecution goes along with
the acceptance of Your Son.
Although symbolic from the start,
the processes moved on to the heart,
a final and true, sweet savor unto You.
You are, were, and will always be
imminently holy.
Raising the question of how You, could
approach someone like me,
feeding me from inspiring words,
that there may be an increase in my reservoir.
Your words be done,
in those I encounter
in days to come.
That is why,
You, God, yearn to approach someone like me.

17

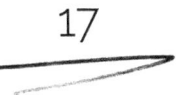

Control of Soul

The enemy wants control.
He wants control of my very soul.
So, I inform my soul
with the Word patrol.
Greater is He who is in me.
That's the One who defends me,
from the one that's outside of me,
who will never guide me.
He really is nobody,
seeking to use my body,
that's already occupied.
He really is nobody,
looking to use your body,
but is it already occupied?
If so, go ahead, testify.
Tell somebody
what He has done,
promising to all
His Kingdom come.
Tell somebody
how He came in,
and delivered you from the dread of sin,
promising to never forsake nor leave,
and throughout eternity vowing to cleave.
Go ahead, tell somebody.

18
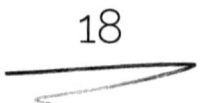

Our Fellowship

That which was from the beginning,
which we have heard,
has now become God's Holy Word.
That which has been seen with our own eyes,
is now handled by the hands of the wise.
I'm speaking of the Word of life,
that eternal life manifested unto us,
that one, Jesus Christ,
that which we have seen and heard,
we declare,
afford our fellowship together anywhere.
Truly, that fellowship with God the Father,
the Son, the Holy One.
So, these things we write unto you,
that your joy may be full and overflowing, too.
This, then, is the measure we have heard of Him.
God is light; in Him is no dim.
If I say I'm in Him, and that I have fellowship,
but in reality, darkness is around me,
I lie.
I lie and do not let the truth reside.
But when I walk in the light,
I have fellowship, one with another so right.
The blood of Jesus Christ, God's Son,
cleanses us from all unrighteous acts done.

If we sin, and we say we have no sin,
we deceive ourselves, with no truth within.
If we confess our sin,
He is faithful, and He is just.
He forgives that sin
and cleanses us, as we trust.
Who can say, "I have made my heart clean,
I am pure from sin"?
Only the one who honors,
first John chapter one, verse nine,
and believes verse ten.
For if and when we have sinned,
and now say we did not sin,
in our thinking,
we make Him a liar, and His Word is not within.
That is the Word;
believe it, you must; that is the Word.
Stick with it and trust.
Soul setting free
will cause us to hear and fear.
Whether issues be far,
far away or so very, very near.

19

God's Way

Quite like the pimple you aggravate,
spewing out the toxin with a rapid migrate.
The process itself can be positive or not so.
But we must be careful where the crud will now go.
When not done meticulously,
it can infect a new territory.
Expulsion so necessary
to relieve pain,
when not performed correctly,
can cause more than a migraine.
And so it is with nasty life issues
that plague you day to day,
getting in your way.
Now, you try to relieve it,
the only way you know,
but there is only one real way:
God's way, the Bible, will show.
Spewing out putrefied gunk,
as you have always done,
will slow down the process
of having that godly result come.
Let the Holy Ghost teach you what to say
at the same hour of that same day.

20

Psalm 43

Psalm forty-three, I love what you say to me.
Judge me, O God, and plead my cause,
according to what You see.
When ungodly people are in control
of this, our nation,
I need You to deliver me from
the ungodly degradation,
the unjust ones,
who love not Your only Son.
You are surely the God of my strength,
the only One I stand stable against.
Giving no place for mourning
because of oppression of the enemy,
who seeks to invade my territory,
You have sent out Your Word,
which is light and truth,
that led me and guided me
through my Christian youth.
You have chosen to tabernacle
with me, Your holy hill,
from which every need
and want You fulfill.

As I go unto the altar of my God,
that's You, with exceeding joy,
my heart is the instrument
of praise to You, O God,
my God, I deploy.
Let me be honest, I will admit,
there are times when I must say,
"Why are you cast down,
"O my soul, this day?"
Me, you will not betray, in any way.
My hope in God will never cease to be
the settling force of liberty.
Praise Him yet I must, for He is the health
of my countenance.
Psalm forty-three,
I love what you say to me.

21

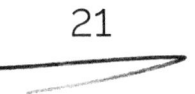

Finish Your Course

Let not the things of life move you from your drive,
to finish your course in Christ.
Count not your life dear to yourself—
leave that for someone else.
Whatever be it, your present condition,
plus or minus provision,
let not that be the force,
to shift you from God's course.
You must believe it is tailored for you,
by Him,
with the express purpose of reaching them.
Let none of these things move you.
Finishing your course with joy is what you do.
Joy unspeakable and full of glory
is what it can always be,
so finish your ministry.
Share the Gospel of His grace,
whether to enemy or friend,
for that is reconciliation,
bringing them to God
for a Father-child relation.
Delay not in declaring God's counsel,
His Word, His testimony,
His Gospel.
Let none of these things move you.
Finish your course with joy too.

Joy, unspeakable and full of glory—
that is what it can always be.
Remember how Paul, in the space of three years,
ceased not to warn everyone night and day with tears?
I, too, commend you to God
and to the Word of His grace,
which is needed to run this race.
God has given to you an inheritance,
among those of us who are sanctified,
for all who fall within that scope of hope,
God will provide.
Let not the things of life
ever move you from the drive
to finish your course in Christ.
Count not your life dear to yourself—
leave that to someone else.

22

Rejoicing

There is always rejoicing in heaven,
over the repenting of one sinner.
There I was, and so did they rejoice,
as I switched from a looser to a winner.
And for me, oh how they did rejoice.
Loudly, I am sure was the boasting of each voice.

Concerning me, that began the devil's defeat.
Yes, that former life had become obsolete.
For anything I've ever lost,
I've turned on the light and swept the floor.
No matter the cost,
I will always diligently seek to find it.
If, by the grace of God,
I see it here or there,
I've just got to go out and tell—
I must make someone else aware.
Likewise, there is joy
in the presence of the angels of God
over one sinner repenting.
YES!
There is joy in the presence of the angels of God
over one sinner relenting.
There is joy!

23

Know His Voice

Let hope be yours
from now until forever.
His voice is heard by me.
I hear it so clearly.
"Go here, go there!"
"Say this, not that."
"Count your blessings!"
"Don't forget."
He speaks so clearly.
I hear, I hear—do You hear me?
Let this hope be yours
from now through infinity.
It's His voice,
and I know it.
Like a sheep and a shepherd,
I know His call.
Where there's a choice
I know His voice.
What He speaks against
I do not follow,
as if it were a pit,
so deep and hollow.
Let this hope be yours
from now until forever,
in all that you endeavor.

Illumination sparks revelation,
providing loads of information.
Placed there in the hearts
of those who love and adore Him.
Where the brightness of the inner most being
Will never again be dim.
So I do, that I do,
I allow hope to be mine,
From now until forever,
each day anew,
and how about you?

24

When Jesus Called

When Jesus called His disciples together,
giving them power
and authority over all devils,
to preach the Kingdom of God . . .
as they continued to trod.

When Jesus called His disciples together,
giving them power
and authority over all devils,
to heal the sick . . .
with Godly power, no cheap trick.

I remember the
appointed seventy—
two by two—Jesus, You
sent them out before Your face
to where You would come,
into every city and place.
For there they would be
surrounded by grace.

So, You said, " when they hear me,
they will hear You.
If they despise me,
they are despising You".
And ditto, too,
they will do to Him
who sent You.

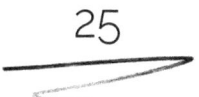

Happy Are We

𝒫ride goes before destruction,
And a haughty spirit comes
before the fall.
So I'll remain with the lowly,
with a humble spirit,
not having to divide the spoil
with the prideful at all.
Much like handling a matter wisely
to find the good,
trusting in the Lord
as I should.
Do you agree?
Then happy are we.

26

Bright Shining Light

There is nothing covered
that will not be revealed.
There is nothing hid
that will remain concealed.
That which is spoken
in the closet, in the darkness,
in the ears at night,
will be again spoken on the housetop,
I promise,
in the bright shining light.

27

Common sense Nonsense

Common sense at times is okay,
but when you compare various issues
to the Word of God,
common sense becomes nonsense.
As in "Paid on time" versus "Paid one time"—
Be it millions or just a dime.
If you are always paying on time,
it's time to change your mind.
Jesus paid one time,
in Sunday school I was taught,
and that's the better thought.
Thank God, there was no need
to string His payments out
through decades and years of time.
I could not have been redeemed
in this life of mine.
Yes, common sense
is nonsense
when you compare it
to the Word of God.

I truly believe it to have been if not the first, then most certainly one of the first three poems given of God. The very essence of this lovely piece of work sprang out of a situation in South Holland, Illinois. Marcel and I have ministered in Kings Community Church, pastored by Pete and Debbie Tassio, for decades.

Pastor Pete received the pastorate following the home going of the founding pastor and our dear friends pastor Bill and Lois Blonde. Not one year have we been apart from either couple. What a lovely body of serious, God-inspired people. Thank you for saying the right thing at the right time, for that was the platform needed to spark that which is below.

28

Ancient of Days

No matter the age you are thus far,
give God the glory for how old you are.
Not one moment of time
was yours to control.
He assigned that
to your angels on patrol.
The older you are, be proud—don't frown
at the sum total years that you've been around.
It's a blessing only our God can give,
so many years He's allowed you to live.

Yell it from the mountaintop as if thunder.
Never cheat God, pretending you are younger,
for the glory locked in
your age
belongs to the Ancient of Days.

All the glory locked in
your age
belongs to the Ancient of Days.

Oh, have you noticed this deception
is almost always delegated
to the self-centered lady?
And I'll throw in
that husky fellow,
so buffed and so mellow.
For there may be a time in your future
when a loved one may accost what you do, "sir,"
as in take your car keys
for the protection of all,
or hide that ladder because of a fall.
However, that in no way
stifles your liberties,
for most of what
was a part
of your life before
is still available—you have
freedom galore.

Yell it from the mountaintop as if thunder.
Never cheat God, pretending you are younger,
for the glory locked in
your age
belongs to the Ancient of Days.
All the glory locked in
your age
belongs to the Ancient of Days.

The more years, the more glory—,
it all tells the story.
All the provision and protection—
what an amazing reflection.
You cannot erase the evidence of time.
He locked it there in the cavern of your mind.
To say else-wise,
you lie to self.
Give God the glory—no one else.

Yell it from the mountaintop as if thunder.
Never cheat God,
pretending you are younger,
for the glory locked in
your age
belongs to the Ancient of Days.
All the glory locked in
your age
belongs to the Ancient of Days.

Now, many have not survived
your number of years.
Their loved ones
have already shed their tears.
But is less time a reason to surmise
that God shortened their stay
and took them away?
That's hidden in glory, as well.
All things of God in the proper time
He will reveal.
But for now, those things are sealed.

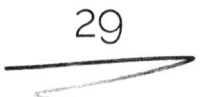

He Found Me

I did not find God—
He was never lost.
He found me.
But how can that be,
when nothing is ever lost from God?
He knows the whereabouts of it all.
I could not have been lost from Him,
not even because of the Fall.
Then what is it
that was found, as if lost?
It was the path back to Him
that was lost to me.
Then I learned the route back
through the death of His Son on the tree.
How lovely!

30

Closer, Much Closer

They who render evil for good
are adversaries of those
who follow the thing that good is.

You are the Lord of my salvation.
You make haste to help me.
You are the Lord of my salvation,
never far from me.

Though the enemies are lively,
though the enemies are strong,
though the enemies may be multiplied,
their action is all wrong.

You are the Lord of my salvation.
You make haste to help me.
You are the Lord of my salvation,
never far from me.

You are closer than Your Word to me,
that Word that nourishes my body.
It keeps me in strength and health.
When needed, it replenishes my wealth.

But You are closer, much closer.
When I speak the Word, it produces for me,
but I don't love You for the things I get to see.
I just love You; I just do.

31

Children of Light

My Father, my God,
Great Master from above,
You are the essence of love.
You are now within,
having forgiven my sin.
I promise to not let
the children of this world,
this generation,
be wiser than we,
Your relation.
the children of light,
that shine so bright.
When we are faithful
in that which is least,
we can become faithful
in all that is right.
You have now committed
to me riches that are true,
and I will retain of it
that which is due.
No servant can serve two masters.
There will be hate for one
and love for another.
We will hold to one and despise the other.
We will not serve God
and mammon, too.
That is one thing
we cannot, will not, do.

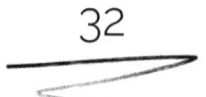

Watch and Pray

*W*atch, therefore, and pray always
to be counted
worthy to escape all these things
that will come to pass.
Desire to stand,
praiseworthy, trustworthy,
before the Son of Man.

33
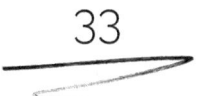

That Kind of Word

This word I need
to be encouraging to me.
That kind of word
is setting my soul free.
That kind of word
causes one to hear and fear
whether far, far away
or so very, very near.
That word!
Who can say, "I have made my heart clean?
"I am pure from sin?"
Only the one who honors First John one nine
and believes verse ten.
For if we say we have not sinned,
we make Him a liar,
and His Word is not within.
That is the word you must stick with,
that word that counters sin.

Mrs. Rose Mitchell: It has been difficult to come forth with words sufficient to express the gratitude that is in our hearts here at Sword and Psalm. So God deemed that we give this poem to you. This is not merely a dedication, but a relenting of what we truly believe was given to us to describe "Rose Mitchell." Do with it what you please, for it now belongs to you.

Mrs. Rose Mitchell

May my God bless you abundantly.
For those unknown to Him
it may seem to be mysteriously.
He is doing what He has always done,
and He always will.
May my God bless you abundantly.

You have fullness of overflowing.
That is affluence—a plentiful amount
is what that's about.
Being independently cared for
is why He is there . . . for
He has blessed you abundantly.

With you, there will be no unlawful use,
as in wrongly, improperly—
I'll just say it—abuse.
The negative thoughts are not in your heart
to trick or to deceive.
My God has blessed you abundantly.

Deceptive, unlawful practice
to secure unfair gain
will at best produce a mockery reign
when my God
has blessed you abundantly.
For those unknown to Him,
it may seem mysteriously.
He's doing what He has always done
and always will.
May my God bless you abundantly.
Yes, He did; yes, He did.
I know that He did.
My God has blessed you abundantly.

We don't need to check
your mode of operation.
It was God who brought it
to culmination.
That's reaching the highest point,
the highest degree,
in this case, monetarily.
My God has blessed you abundantly.
Yes, He did; yes, He did.
I know that He did.
Yes, He did.
Yes, He did.
Yes, He did.

When it comes to the Word of God, my favorite teacher is "the man—my man," Marcel Joseph Jr. I am not being biased, just telling the truth! Well, I needed to say that because the next in line was inspired by that all-time loving man of mine.

35

Looking Back

You can't tell me this is not true.
Looking back will stifle you.
But looking back is not the problem,
without a doubt.
It's remembering back
that I am talking about.
The back of anything
that you cannot go through
is the farthest from the front.
Don't waste your time on that junk.
Whatever happened way back there
is not worthy of today's time and care—
especially if you are looking
to go somewhere.
Your present situation
may need some prayer.
Go ahead, look forward
from here to there.
Don't be surprised
if what you envisioned
has now become today's provision.

Looking back is not worth your time and delay.
Looking forward will reward;
it's profitable and will pay.
Continue looking forward from this day,
and you will have exactly what you say.
I say I'm sealed,
healed,
blessed.
I'm God-possessed.

Don't wait for the event to begin.
Do your part to help usher it in.
Go ahead and look forward
from here to there.
You will surely live it, being firmly aware,
looking forward from this day,
you'll have exactly what you say.
I say I am sealed,
healed,
blessed,
I'm God-possessed.
I am blessed.

36

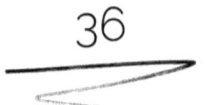

Rock of Ages

We all need noise about
how He is in our heart
at all times, not just a part.
He gives constant rest,
as He is always the same.
He made it so
that we find grace in His name.
The solid Rock of Ages He will always be—
that solid Rock of Ages we will always need.
Rock of Ages He will always be,
that sure, firm Rock
that was cleft for me.
While in my spirit You reside,
without a location to run and hide,
You chose the only place to resort,
providing love, providing support.
We ourselves restrict not to appear,
before You, Lord our God,
throughout the year.
We forsake not the assembling of ourselves together,
needed for the fellowship of one another,
no matter the weather.
Rock of Ages, You will always be
that sure firm Rock,
that was cleft for me.

37

Victory

The great temptations
that your eyes see,
signs, wonders,
that mighty,
stretched-out hand—that's victory.
He brought you out, and He always will.
Your godly desires, He will fulfill.
Do not be affrighted,
for your God is mighty.
The Lord your God is among us
and in you.
A mighty God, and terrible, too.

As we reflect on past happenings, we can agree they are not always good. However, we cannot lean on the things of the future to strengthen us. There is no substance there—it has not happened yet. Often in life, we look back at the good and bad, many times extracting solace. Only then are we able to make the adjustments, the corrections needed, to be empowered. My desire is that this next "National Reminder" will, indeed, put the supply into that need.

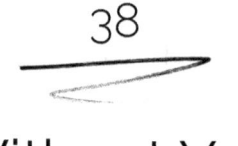

38

Without You

Good morning, Father.
How wonderful to know You are never bothered.
My question today is—
Let me say—
How do people do this world without You?
When investigating their day in the a.m., maybe let's say at two,
At that early hour, will they know what to do?
Pondering issues that make them wonder and worry,
breathing upon the soon-coming hours of the day,
indeed, making them blurry
Hey, God!
How do people do this world without You?
On this day, March twenty-seven, twenty and twenty-three,
I heard a newsfeed.
The assailant, they say a transvestite,
did an act of travesty,
canceling out lives in Nashville, Tennessee.
As she came prepared, she had a gun.
It is said she had more than one.

Lives were brought to an abrupt end,
purposelessly by the hand of another,
and it makes you wonder.
Did she have a father, a mother?
Did she have a sister?
Did she have a brother?
Likely she did, but what I do know
is what her very actions show.
She was minus in her knowledge
and love for You, Father,
and it's much too late
to correct that horror.
What I will say is, thank You, Father,
for the life You gave to each afflicted one
who was snuffed out that day
in such a horrible display.
Thank You for what each one
was able to contribute,
although, for the most part,
they were all so very young,
to not leave out, not even one.
What they were able to achieve
will not be forgotten,
will not be undone.
So, how do people do this world
without You, Father?
Not very well,
actions like this tell.

39

In His Image

God created man in His image.
In the image of God created He him.
Male and female created He them.

Then God blessed them, saying,
"Be fruitful and multiply.
"This earth subdue, replenish,
"dominate the fish of the sea,
"the fowl of the air, every living thing
"that is there.
"Dominate the herb,
"trees bearing seed, all yielding feed.
"All for you to enjoy; it is you I employ."
God, seeing all that He had made,
uttered, "Good, so good, so very good."

O Lord God, how excellent You are.
You have granted me life and favor.
Your visitation preserved my spirit,
decreased my efforts of labor.
I came out when You came in,
seeing the light that exposed the sin.
From that landmark day,
whenever there is sin,
You acquit me of my iniquity.

I will not be wicked, no woes will come unto me,
and lifted high my head will be.
I'll not submit to fusion,
confusion, nor illusion.

There is an enemy out there,
I'm very aware,
who wants to relate, sedate,
and then migrate.
But he'll never settle in me;
it will never be,
for I am already occupied,
and He who is in me
is not there to hide.
Oh my, His visitation
preserved my spirit.
Full of goodness within,
never burdened with
thought to sin.
I withhold no good
from those to whom it is due
when it is in the power of my hand
to let flow through.
I say not to my neighbor, "Go,
"and come again,"
when I have it then.
Devise evil against no one.
Strive not with man—that's never fun.
Those who oppress, I envy not,
nor do I choose the maze
of their ways.

Lord, You bless as You must
the habitation of the just.
And while the earth remains—
seedtime, harvest,
summer and winter,
cold and heat,
day and night, will not cease.

Because God created man in His image.
In the image of God created He him.
Male and female created He them.

40

Privileged Bunch

There is a storm going on out there somewhere.
I don't hear thunder, nor do I see lightning.
However, I will take care.

I'm living a quiet and peaceable life,
amidst strife.
That is the promise He gave,
while in my heart I saved.
I'm speaking it forth with a loud shout,
and I'm watching Him carry it out.

I've got my promise, and I'm living a quiet life.
The enemy won't win with his dirty old strife.
He's foiled again; he can't win.
I don't play around with his sin.
I'm in a privileged bunch.
You can't talk me down, because I have found
the most privileged bunch around.
That is what the life of a Christian's about.

The last chapter of Acts is not the end,
and we are to continue, my friend.
You'll never get me to speak unadvisedly.
I know exactly what He said to me.
He said I can live a quiet life—
a quiet life amidst strife.

Quiet is calm and unmoving—
you may even think it's soothing.
There could also be little or no sound,
but in the confines of this poem,
the enemy can't harass or hound.
When they annoy repeatedly,
as they persist trying to
wear another out,
and that is the power
of what strife is about.
That is the life we won't have to live,
the one our God did not give.

I've got a promise, and I'm living a quiet life.
The enemy is not winning
with his dirty old strife.
He's foiled again; he can't win.
I don't play around with his sin.

I'm in a privileged bunch.
You can't talk me down
because I have found
the most privileged bunch around.

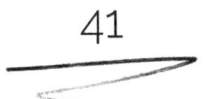

Run, Walk, Talk

We entered this universe
neither walking, nor talking.
Yet, this, that, and another we all pursue.
Throughout the Word,
we are told just what to do.
Continue to listen
and let me inform you.
It's in the Spirit, if you can believe it,
that we run, walk, talk.

There is a plan to develop that ability,
growing from pauper to royalty.
We're walking and talking
our way through to victory,
considering the depth
of our prosperity, hilariously.

Throughout the Word,
we are told just what to do.
Continue to listen, and let me inform you.
It's in the Spirit, if you can believe it,
that we run, walk, talk.
Nothing corrupt do I ever want to speak.
It will not proceed.
It will not release.
I proclaim that my words are good.
They edify and minister grace, as they should.
Communicating is main with a Christian.

Talking is not mundane when others listen.
Continue to listen, and let me inform you.
It's in the Spirit, if you can believe it,
that we run, walk, talk.
Talking reflects all that we say.
Walking involves what we do
in the course of our day.
When we stay within the boundary
of the Word we have heard,
that's walking on higher ground,
and not all have found.
You are now in that place
where others will listen to you, too.
Inform them of this or that,
how and when to do.

It's in the Spirit, if you can believe it,
that we run, walk, talk.

Walking reflects what we do.
Running depicts how we do it—swiftly to the end.
No longer walking, but running, my friend,
to the absolute end.

We entered this universe
neither walking, nor talking.
Yet this, that, and another, we all pursue.
Throughout the Word,
we are all told just what to do.
Continue to listen,
and let me inform you.
It's in the Spirit,
if you can believe it.
We run, walk, talk.

The Word Has Set You F-r-e-e

With the Word in you,
and the anointing upon you, too,
There's still one thing you can't do.
Though you name it,
and/or you claim it,
you can't reap it,
if you didn't speak it.
Don't even seek it.
Give the Word a chance
to bring it to pass.

To desire outside His boundary
is a trap set by the enemy.
That forbidden ground to you is not free.
It will cost part of your liberty.
Don't give up any
of what in Him you've gained!
You'll need it all for your future,
So, just let it remain.
If it's not for you,
then don't desire to.
Just flee to higher ground.
Do you feel uneasy?
Then flee to higher ground.
Hearing a different sound?
Then flee to higher ground.

If you run today,
you will live tomorrow.
Then you will look back
upon that trek of horror.
You will have escaped the trap set for you.
God knew you would and allowed you to,
while all the time He watched over you.
Look around, now that's familiar ground.
You can come on up
to where you are supposed to be,
with no more deceit.
The Word has set you free.
If you run this day, you will live tomorrow.
The Word has set you free.
Yes, free.
F-R-E-E.
The Word has set you free.
You are not in prison or enslaved.
You are not affected or limited by a specific craze.
There are many words,
compounded with free,
you'll see.
Free agent, free form, free hand.
Freeport, free load, free stand.
Freeway, free trade, free enterprise,
that's wise.
Free thinker, free fall.
Free spoken, free for all.
But the frees I like the best,
much better than all the rest,
are free born, free man,
as in you and me.

Free reign, free-hearted,
as in Father, Son, Holy Ghost,
the three-divinity over me.
How about a free ride?
You don't pay for salvation.
You just decide.
Free will, it's all up to you.
You're not hypnotized,
as in mesmerized.
Yes, the Word has set us free.
F-R-E-E.
The Word has set us free.
To desire outside His boundary
is a trap set by the enemy.
That forbidden ground to you is not free,
and it will cost you part of your liberty.
If you run this day,
you will live tomorrow.
Flee to higher ground.

43

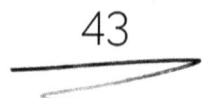

You're the Apple of God's Own Eye

Crisis and his partner, called chaos,
will daily drain your wealth until it's all lost,
at all costs,
leaving you disturbingly delusional
when for you that is highly unusual,
because you are the apple of God's own eye.
Being prone like a fetus is no position for you.
The Word gives strength,
So, stand tall as you go through
what seems to be defeat.
You will not be the one to retreat.
You are the apple of God's own eye.
We may see you give a wink and later hear a sigh,
but you are still the apple of God's own eye.
When we are rejected,
there's no need to be dejected.
Why be marked by that low spirit?
Be it depression or oppression,
that is a state of delusion.
And I've concluded,
I am the apple of God's own eye.
Oh my, I am the apple of God's own eye.
Why cry?

Apple is a fruit we all know,
but I'll not allow it to steal the show.
There is a much deeper thought,
we must not miss.
Please be patient
while I take you through this.

One definition for *apple* is "pupil", that circular aperture
through which light enters the eye
is known as the pupil.
This bit of insight is crucial.
Although you may not have noticed,
whenever someone stands before you,
their image can be seen by them,
reflecting from your eyes—
give it a try.
And it is so with you, as well,
I do tell.
But the most thought-provoking occasion came
when God spoke my name,
saying to me that I am the apple of His own eye.
I am the *apple* of His *pupil*, oh my.
As we stand before God, our Savior,
our image is within Him, reflected in His pupil.
We are legally there,
be it in praise, worship, or prayer,
as He deemed us suitable.
At those times, we are
the apple, or more accurately the pupil,
of God's own eye,
oh my!

Well, now it is time to get back,
to the original thought
as it is time for the ending.
And that takes us all the way back
to the beginning.

Crisis and his partner called chaos
will daily drain your wealth until it's all lost,
at all costs,
leaving you disturbingly delusional
when for you that is highly unusual
because you are the apple of God's own eye.
Now we are back on track
and you may need to pinch yourself
as you march toward wealth.
That's okay, I'm allowed to say.
It will affect no one but you
as you follow through.
There will be an increase
that occasionally follows a release.
Is it not better to give than to receive?
The pain and shame of others relieve?
After all, they are the apple of God's own eye, oh my!
They are the apple of God's own eye . . . solidify,
give it a try.
Don't wonder why—
it's not a lie.
They are the apple of God's own eye.

44

More Than Gold

*L*et the words of my mouth,
and the meditation of my heart,
be acceptable in Thy sight, O Lord,
my strength and my Redeemer.
More to be desired are they than gold,
providing peace and comfort for the very soul.
Day unto day utters speech,
night unto night knowledge released.
There is no speech or language,
where the sound is never heard.
Out through all the earth goes the spoken word.
To even the end of the world
is that sound hurled.
More to be desired are they than gold,
providing peace and comfort for the very soul.

The law of the Lord is perfect, converting the soul,
changing the worst of the worst, I'm told,
to the best of the best of all the rest.
The testing of the Lord is sure,
with much power to allure,
making wise the simple,
in preparation of their temple.
More to be desired are they than gold,
providing peace and comfort for the very soul.

The statutes of the Lord are right,
rejoicing the heart.
Removing all heaviness to make light that part.

The commandment of the Lord is pure,
enlightening the eyes
of those who were blind,
and of the not so wise.
The fear of the Lord is clean
and endures forever,
helping you to remain,
departing never.
More to be desired are they than gold,
providing peace and comfort for the very soul.

The judgment of the Lord is true
and righteous all together,
providing more freedom,
having released from the tether.
Let the words of my mouth,
and the meditation of my heart
be acceptable in Thy sight,
O Lord, my strength and my Redeemer.

More to be desired are they than gold,
providing peace and comfort for my very soul.

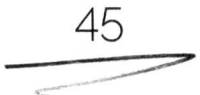

Good and Upright Are You

$\mathcal{S}$howing me Your ways,
teaching me Your paths,
leading me in truth,
You remember me,
with tender mercies.
Loving-kindnesses too,
good and upright are You.
My soul will dwell at ease,
for I am Your seed.
I forsake doing what I please.
Integrity will preserve me,
for uprightness will not flee.
You will keep my soul and deliver me;
That is autonomy.
It is what You do
good and upright are You.

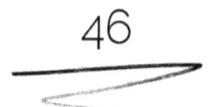

46

Seedling

The Word is much like a seed.
It takes time to spawn a root.
Then sometimes after,
we enjoy delectable fruit.
The underground part of a plant
serves as support,
drawing water and food of some sort.
The seed is the primary source,
the beginning of what is to be—
maybe a number of objects,
hanging from a tree.
The origin of a thing
is the most important,
for without it,
there could never be a thing,
don't doubt it.
That could be the most misfortunate.
You must plant a seed indeed.
Never cease to strive to be the one,
to sow the Word.
Take it from me, for I have shouted
when the fruit occurred.
You have to believe to sow,
before what you sow can grow,
is all I know.

47

I Give Thanks to You

Lord, I'm not offering oblations to You,
from the wilderness of Sinai.
But on my knees bended,
I'm coming to You
with needs I cannot deny.
The stone which the builders rejected
is now the head of the corner.
This was the Lord's doing,
marvelous in the eyes of the wise,
the owner.
I give thanks to You.
You have turned for me
my mourning into dancing.
I go about running, leaping,
now even prancing.
You have my sackcloth.
You dressed me with gladness.
To that end, my soul sings
praises of kindness.
I give thanks to You forever.
As I place my head
in a position to nod,
I will not be silent,
O Lord my God.
I give thanks to You anew.

My zeal for God is measured
by my knowledge of Him.
Being ignorant of even one attribute
will cause me to falter in that pursuit.
We serve a credible God,
who is to be believed
at all times, not now and then,
thereby eliminating that question of when.
I give thanks to You forever.
You are the Lord of all,
who is rich unto all,
to all who call upon Your name,
who were affected by the Fall.
For whosoever will call on
the Lord will be saved,
no matter the season,
no matter the reason.
Him only do we praise.
As I place my head
in a position to nod.
I will not be silent,
O Lord my God.
I give thanks to You anew.
I give thanks anew to You.

He Brought Me Through

I don't have to see with my eyes
Jesus, walking on the sea.
I'd rather be wise, let Him guide,
He is living here in me.
I'm no longer sore,
amazed in myself beyond measure.
And to wonder would take away from the rising pleasure.

Good and upright is He.
I go back and consider
the miracle of the loaves,
an image my heart shows:
the paw of the lion;
the paw of the bear.
I best not forget—no, no,
I don't ever dare.
He brought me through, you'd better know.
He brought me through.
Waiting on You, Lord, is mine to do.
O my God, how I trust in You.

I will not be ashamed.
All Your promises are "yes" and "amen,"
and that I have already claimed.
He brought me through.
I won't ever forget Your miracle of the loaves.

Whatever it may have been,
for and if, you do and when,
there will be no fading memory,
of how He brought you the victory.
That regression will not help to push
you forward in the battle you face today.
If you were delivered from the paw of the lion,
the paw of the bear,
it is best you do not forget.
Don't you dare.

There will come a time when you'll hear the words,
"Be not afraid.
"Be of good cheer.
"It is I; it is I,
"be not afraid.
"Remember how on Calvary you were delivered.
"I paid, I paid.
"Be not afraid.
"Every miracle will lay strength in the platform
"for the next need that will arise.
"It is I; it is I,
"I paid, I paid.
"Be not afraid."
He brought you through, yes.
Don't ever forget.
There is no reason to doubt.
He brought you out.

49

Joy and Glory

The prospering of the Word
that you have received is up to you.
Where and how you plant seed
is left up to you, too.
If it falls by the wayside,
the fowls of the air will not hide.
In their time to sup,
they swoop down and gobble it up.
But my story is filled with joy and glory.
Joy and glory,
that's my story.

Be mindful of stony ground.
Take time to look around.
Where there is not sufficient earth
for the seed to birth,
it will spring up quickly,
but with no secure root,
becoming sun-withered swiftly.
What if your seed is thrown among thorns,
which grow up and choke out life before fruit is born?
That all sounds like a sad, sad ending to life.
It should not be our plight.
We will plant properly,
for joy and glory for a better story.

The seed of the Word that falls on God's ground
will yield fruit as high as a mound.
Springing up, it will increase, bringing forth
some thirty-, some sixty-, some a hundredfold, of course.
That's my story, filled with joy and glory,
Joy and glory,
that's my story,
That's my story,
these days and always.

I've Got a Promise

I've got a promise from God, my Father.
He spoke this to me:
I've more than enough.
It's called authority.
I just won't do and don't want to,
trying to keep the pace,
when I should die to,
not be tied to,
the same old race.

He said I'm above and not beneath.
That is enough for the enemy's defeat.
I'm not tied down,
don't have to turn around,
I've got a promise.
I'm facing that foe
who's got to get up and go.
I've got a promise from God, my Father.
He spoke this to me:
I've got more than enough with my authority.
I'm not backing down.
My feet on solid ground,
I've got a promise.

If anybody's backing down, it won't be me.
That foe never wants to be around
when to God I show loyalty.
I've got a promise.
I don't have any kind of relationship
with any enemy of my Savior.
My battles are already won,
thanks to God's Son.
All that the enemy is playing out is mock,
I've got a promise.

He's not my match.
There will be no tie,
because nothing will be going on
between him and I.
There is nothing between
the devil and anyone of concern to me,
I decree,
nothing befitting, nothing civil.
I've got a promise.

I'm of the state of the Kingdom of God.
It's already done.
I'm God's citizen,
opposed to the devil's community.
I've pledged my allegiance to God's military,
God's organized society.
I've got a promise.
Whatever the devil is trying to do is trivial,
a relatively insignificant matter.
Why would I quiver, shake or quake, or shatter?
I've got a promise.

He's not competitive; he's just a pursuer.
All tactics are old; none are newer.
Wanting to capture or overtake
is the way he and his imps relate.
He wants to continue to carry on,
but what he did have here is already gone,
and that was ME.
Now, that's my victory.
I've got a promise.

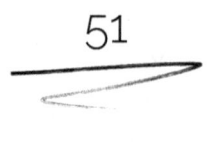

My Echo

Baptism was a sign
that I had done what
I had heard or read,
that having been
what God had said,
making the statement that I was saved,
when early on, I had not learned to behave.
This is my echo,
the repeating of an act that will never end.
There will be no need to do it again.
The day I denounced sin
was the day Jesus announced me as friend.
Neither He nor I will ever rescind.
No need for a second dunk
that can only imitate the other
with no more power or authority,
so, no need for another.

Do enjoy what comes next, as it was truly inspired, by the old Christian hymn "O the Blood of Jesus, It Washes White as Snow."

He Washed Us White as Snow

He washed us white as snow.
Now we all know.
He washed us white as snow.
"White" in no way references
the absence of pigmentation
we may or may not see,
but it is the ultimate, never-ending presence
of godly purity.
He washed us white as snow.
Now we all know.
He washed us white as snow.
The white that the song highlights
only beams from inside.
There is no switch to flick it on or off,
indicating something to hide.
He washed us white as snow,
Now we all know.
He washed us white as snow.
Everything dark and dreary came out then,
but when?
As He forgave us of all that sin.
You see, He was always destined
to move Himself in.

But it was not until then
that He did wash us white as snow.
You can't blow the horn in Zion
when you've failed to blow it in your heart,
and with your mind, will, and intellect, from evil depart.
Maybe the soul will for a while go on chilling.
But the spirit, at that point,
will always be willing
to do God's Word
exactly as heard,
with great resurge.
White is the achromatic color of maximum lightness,
having zero saturation, no hue, though some brightness.
It is the compliment or antagonist of black and
when the mindset is to oppose and actively compete,
as neither side wants to suffer defeat,
but that is the worldly thought,
not the white coming from the heart.
Words like *Caucasoid, Negroid and Mongoloid*
are of no significance when considering salvation,
as they are combinedly the same when considering relations
Where the B-i-b-l-e majors, we will major, too.
Where there is a minor, we k-n-o-w what to do.
Because He washed us white as snow. Now we all know.
He washed us white as snow.
Black being of the darkest,
achromatic visual value,
producing or reflecting comparatively
little light and having almost no hue too,
as in white,
little or no light.
black and stormy night.

From the biblical side,
Nothing here to hide.
He washed us white as snow
Now we all know

Little significance on this subject
in the Word of God,
none of which comes over odd.
I thank God that salvation is free.
There is no cost to you or me.
Yes, set apart from all differences,
it holds true, too, in deliverances.

For sure, He washed us white as snow.
We all now know.
He washed us white as snow.
But you must share this with those,
Who do not know.

53

Be Aware

We are a nation great, mighty and populous.
Goodness and mercy follows after us.
We will not be evil entreated, afflicted,
under any kind of bondage.
You won't block us up nor weigh us down,
 with words of worthless correspondence.
You will not impede or hinder.
The burden you seek to put in place,
will not interfere with our power.
We will continue to lead in this race.

Those who attempt to afflict, bear labor or oppression, be aware.
We cry unto the Lord God, our Father,
who hears our voice because He does care.
What He did before in history
He will do for us with that same mighty hand
and outstretched arm.
Be not amazed as we suffer no harm.
There will be great terribleness,
with signs and wonders,
but we are in this place He gave us,
and we'll not go under.
All His decisions are just.
We are protected by His hand.

We are the mighty, mighty band
He brought into this place.
He gave us this land,
To rest during this race.

The Lord is our Shepherd.
We shall not want.
He allows us to lie where our pasture is green,
leading us beside waters that stream.
Depicting the feed of our never-ending need,
the Lord is our Shepherd.
He's restored our soul.
Led to paths of righteousness,
we will forever confess
His name, to us He gave.
To this, none can contest,
nor level a bona-fide protest.
Depicting conversion, we are not ashamed
to confess Christianity.
We in Him, and He in us,
That is our strength and ability
so tell the world we must.
We say it again, "He is in us".
The Lord is our Shepherd.
As we walk through the valley of the shadow of death,
we do not fear evil
for He is with us,
we trust.
Depicting His protection,
that never-ending comfort is our thrust.

The Lord is our Shepherd.
A table He has prepared
where our enemy can see,
we are anointed; the oil runs free.
Surely goodness, surely mercy follows after us.
That is why our nation is great, mighty, and populous.
We will not be evil entreated, afflicted,
under any kind of captivity,
instead walking forth in godly liberty.
We will not be encumbered.
They won't block us up, weigh us down.
The burden they seek to put in place will not impede or hinder.
Nor will we, at any time, to the enemy surrender.
We are empowered to continue to lead in this race.
Those who try to afflict, bear labor and oppression, be aware.
We cry unto the Lord God, our Father, who hears
our voice because He does care.

54

Dig It–Dung It

When a tree is not producing,
time after time after time,
should we cut it down
since it seems to only encumber the ground?
Patience, my friend.
Don't rush to the end.
For now, let us just keep it around.
Dig it–dung it,
as you were told,
and in the proper time,
fruit you will hold.

What seems to be dysfunctional
could become a powerful shoot,
with an earth-piercing root,
as it begins to grow and produce.
That is what I chose to deduce.
So, dig it–dung it,
as you were told in the proper time,
and fruit you will hold.
Collectable,
delectable,
nothing to reject.
No throwaways, spit-outs,
nothing to discard.
What a reward!

All because you recognized the quality of the tree
and refused to destroy it in infancy.

The lesson here?
Wherever there is life,
always accept.
It's worth pondering in depth.
Deny the thought to not give affection,
or recognition to that which strives to be alive.
Dig it–dung it,
as you were told in the proper time,
life you will hold.
It's in your control.

55

You Three Have Entered In

Thank You, precious Spirit of God,
my Comforter,
for Your important part.
Oh, how You sealed,
and You also revealed,
my Father God's gracious heart.

My Father, Provider, Resider,
You let me be, and see
what You have in store for me.
The depth of Your blessings have no end.
My causes, though sometimes great,
You defend.

Dear Jesus, my Brother and Friend,
You made all things possible.
Without Your surrender,
how could we give in?
Our life's cycle would have come to its end,
Jesus, my Brother and Friend.
You three have entered in.

The three of You suffered evenly,
with not even one regret.
The requirement for You to enter me
most surely was already met.

So, I lift my hands and love on You three,
not one more than another.
The salvation plan laid forth by Your hands
has now been uncovered.

Thank You, precious Spirit of God,
my Comforter.
Thank You, dear Jesus, my Brother and Friend,
for You three have entered in.
Again,
You three have entered in.

The three of You suffered evenly, with not even one regret.
The means for You to enter me most surely was already met.
Thank You, precious Spirit of God,
my Comforter.
Thank You, my Father, Provider, Resider.
Thank You, dear Jesus, my Brother and Friend,
for You three have entered in.
I'll say it again:
You three have entered in.

We Must (Retain)

Moses and Aaron heard God's demand.
Went to Pharaoh to lay out the plan.
Saying, "The God of the Hebrews has met with us.
"Three days into the desert to worship, we must,
"to sacrifice before the God whom we trust, we must."

God said, "Let My people go."
But Pharaoh said, "No, no, no!
"Who is the Lord that I should obey His voice.
"I know not Him.
"I won't let the people go, go, go.
"I'll not release them.
"No, no, no!
"I won't let the people go."
So, Pharaoh said, "Not this day,
"I can't let them go, no way."

Then God said, "Tell that Pharaoh,
"The God of the Hebrews said, 'If you refuse and hold them still,
"'you will be holding them against their will.
"'The hand of the Lord be upon animals in the field.
"'None belonging to Israel will I kill.
"'Tomorrow, will I do this thing in the land.'"
And God followed through with His plan.
Because Pharaoh did not give,
the cattle died; they did not live.

What Israel owned remained alive.
Believe me, they all survived.

God said, "Tell that Pharaoh,
"'The God of the Hebrews said to let go.'"
Moses and Aaron, upon
God's request,
took ashes from the furnace—
what a mess!
Standing before Pharaoh,
they sprinkled before the sky,
causing boils upon man
and animals—oh my!
Because the magicians were covered, as well,
there was nothing of that issue they could foretell.

Again, God said, "Tell that Pharaoh,
"'The God of the Hebrews said to let go.'"
God had to harden the heart of Pharaoh,
once again, though.
Early in the morning, Moses stood before the man,
warning him of God's demand:
"Because you exalt yourself against My people
"and will not let them go,
"tomorrow this time
"I will cause it to rain hail
"that in comparison of
"all other times, will certainly pale."
The following day, as God had said,
hail visited, mingled with fire,
producing God's desire.

Smote in the field,
man and beast
destroyed every herb,
broke every tree.
Daily in the land of Goshen,
where the children of Israel lived,
there was no hail to God's avail.
The Hebrews did prevail.
The heart of Pharaoh was hardened once again,
as well as the heart of his servants,
women and men.
So that they may tell in the ears of their son and son's son,
what things God had done.
Moses and Aaron
went and entered in,
saying to him,
in the brightness of day—
it was not dim—
"This is from the God of the Hebrews.
"How long will you refuse?
"Let My people go
"that they may serve Me.
"Set My people free."
God said, "Let My people go.
"If not, I will bring in the locusts.
"Not one in your kingdom
"will not lose their focus."
All was said and done,
but Pharaoh would not be won.
Moses stretched the rod over Egypt,
and locusts appeared in one humongous swoop.

Grievous were they in the loop.
Is that not what the Lord did say?
This is now payday.
Pharaoh called for Moses and Aaron in a haste,
not much time to waste.
Out of his mouth, he uttered these words,
which all heard.
"I have sinned against the Lord again.
"Entreat your God that my sin will end."

Moses went from Pharaoh and did so.
Swiftly he did go.
The Lord sent a mighty wind,
to bring it to an end.
Although He had forgiven the sin,
still God hardened again Pharaoh's heart.
The express purpose of Him doing this part,
we cannot exclude the three days of darkness,
when Moses put out his hand
toward heaven once again.
All over Egypt, it was darker than dark.
AMEN!
But the children of Israel in their dwelling had light,
so bright.
Pharaoh spoke as though he would release them,
but that fell through,
as Moses' demands were much more grand
and God hardened Pharaoh's heart,
there, where he did stand.

Pharaoh said, "No, no, no,
"who is the Lord that I should obey His voice?

"I know not this God.
"I won't let the people go, go, go.
"No, no, no.
"I won't let the people go."
So, Pharaoh said, "Not this day,
"I can't let them go—no way."

The Lord gave His people much favor,
in the sight of all Egyptians.
None threw a conniption.
"Speak now in the ears of the people
"Jehovah's command.
"From all the people in all the land,
"borrow of your neighbor,
"every woman, every man,
"jewels of silver and gold.
"It is foretold."
Moses then said,
"Thus said the Lord,
"'Around midnight I will go into the midst of Egypt,
"'Listen up.
"'All the firstborn in the land will die,
"'Do not be surprised.
"'Beginning at Pharaoh's house
"'to the firstborn of maidservants,
"'to the firstborn of all the beasts,
"'much like a slaughter feast.
"'But against none of the children of Israel,
"'will a dog move his tongue—
"'against no one,
"'not man or beast,
"'from this they are released.

"'Then you will know
"'how the Lord put a difference
"'between you and them,
"'from the top of the head
"'to the bottom of the hem.'"
Now Moses explained to all
how to prepare for protection.
Any household could have opted out;
it was their election.
He went through it step by step.
That he did, yep!
Preparation was to be made
after instructions were laid.
The last thing was to take of the blood,
applying up the sides and over the door and above,
like a flood.
This would become the basis of the
Passover meal.
More than sustenance was taken in.
God provided a protective seal.
The blood was a token
on the houses where they were,
no matter how near or far.
He said, "When I see the blood,
"I will pass over you.
"You will not be destroyed."
What a loving promise—oh, what joy!
"This day will be to you as a memorial
"that, in all times will never be forgotten,
"how your escape from Egypt was begotten.
"It will be a feast to the Lord
"throughout all nations of all generations."

57

He Said, He Saw

He said He is the God of the universe,
that to myself I did rehearse
over, and over, and over again.
Until I believed Him,
I could not receive Him.

That other voice I heard in contrary
wanted to confuse, misuse, and subdue.
I didn't believe that chat,
so, I turned my back on that.
With him my spirit could not renew.
I don't have to plead
when I fall on my knees,
but I cried, "Come into my heart,
"and now do Your part.
"Jesus is Your only Son.
"He died for me on that tree."
When I said it
and believed it,
He saw my heart.
He received it.
I am now His child,
and it didn't take a while.
It happened immediately.
He said He's the God of the universe.
That, to myself, I continue to rehearse,

Over, and over, and over again,
morning, noon, and night,
as I pray.
To my heart's desire, I say,
"I am who You say I am,
"I have what You say I have.
"I can do what You say to do.
"I can be what You decree.
"I can go where You send me,
"be all that I need to be,
"gain all that You have for me,
"give wherever I am directed,
"to whomever You have selected."

He Did, He Did It, He Died

If Jesus did not go to hell for all humanity,
then take my word,
believe you me,
what you think He did not do
will then never be done.
Not ever by anyone

But He did, He did it, He died.
Descended into the deep,

won the battle
that canceled our defeat.
Doing it for you,
doing it for me,
that is what He did.
So, that thought cannot be valid,
given that great defeat.
But be it unto you according to your faith.
This important issue *is* up for debate.
I thank my God,
it will not bar you from heaven's gate.
The one and only absolute way to fail,
is to not give confession of birth,
death, and resurrection,
made ready by Jesus,
that must prevail.

59

Damsel, Arise

Spoken by our Lord,
"Why make you this ado and weep?
"The damsel is not dead, but asleep."
They laughed Him to scorn,
and He put them all out.
Took the father and mother,
alone with the Three,
and entered the room for victory.
Took the damsel by the hand,
and said, "Arise."
That she did.
What a surprise
for those on the outside.

60

How Can It Be?

How can it be, Lord,
that You are speaking to me?
Oh! Jesus, You made it possible,
I read it in the Gospel.
That book is so immutable.
It will never be refutable.
Those who try
to deny its accuracy
are left slapped in the face with truth,
confessing how they now see.
There is no greater script
for the solving of all the world's perplexities.
Where there is doubt,
the Word will work it out.
We are all apt to change;
susceptible to adjustment,
we can rearrange.
Before the action comes,
by God's dictates,
the inevitable event
is predestined by His fate.

61

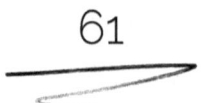

I'll Speak for You

I'll speak for You, Lord.
I'll speak for You, Lord.
I'll do for You, Lord,
I'll follow through.

There's a bubbling sense
of Him welling up in me,
compelling me to follow through,
so how can I not do?
And of that, I will never regret, nor fret.

I'll speak for You, Lord.
I'll do for You, Lord,
I'll follow through.

You are the God of all good,
and You will always exist.
Now, who am I to challenge and resist?
When You say it,
I'll relay it or replay it
without a doubt.
I'll relay it or replay it;
I won't cast it out.

I'll speak for You, Lord.
I'll do for You, Lord,
I'll follow through.
With this clinging presence,
what do I do
to cast aside the hindrance
and follow You?
It's You and me, Lord—
What a perfect fit.
I can't wrap my mind around
what it would be like to quit.
You are the God of all good
and perfect things.
And how wise,
giving me confidence that can only rise.

I'll speak for You, Lord.
I'll do for You, Lord,
I'll follow through.
You are the God
no man can come near.
Out of respect for You, I do fear.

When you say it,
I'll relay it,
or
replay it.
Without a doubt,
I'll relay it or replay it.
I won't cast it out.
I'll speak for You.

62

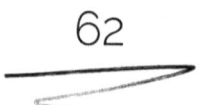

The Ingredient

Do you have honor, an honest report?
Are you full of wisdom,
full of the Holy Ghost?
He is the ingredient
that's bound to work.
Being filled with His Spirit will never hurt.
He is love, He is joy, sensitivity,
as He moves you on to maturity.
Your costly possessions may only be gold-plated.
Don't look down your nose—
remember when you didn't have those?
The wisdom, my friend,
is in your ability
to be faithful with what you get for security.
Are you full of wisdom,
full of the Holy Ghost?
He is the ingredient,
you need the most.
That's bound to work.
Being filled with His Spirit will never hurt.
A little here, a little there,
you may not think it's fair,
but your attitude will determine
the level of quality of your future wealth.
Not only that, but even your health.
Being pressured to grow too fast is not good.

Being tempted to do
what you never thought you would.
Are you full of wisdom,
full of the Holy Ghost?
He is the ingredient,
you need the most.
That's bound to work.
Being filled with His Spirit will never hurt.
The Holy Ghost will help you stay behind the lines.
Boundaries can be your friend, you will realize,
Before long, you'll start to see, a little here, a little there, is not all bad.
It's far more than you ever had.
Now you're in the right mode you appreciate,
and you are financially eager
to participate.

Are you full of wisdom,
full of the Holy Ghost?
He is the ingredient, you need the most.

That's bound to work.
Being filled with His Spirit will never hurt.
He is love, He is joy, sensitivity,
as He moves you on to maturity
Now, I'm not against a chunk at a time.
A windfall blessing will help move you up that line.
Just let Him do it.
Don't you pursue it.
That's all fine.
A little here, a little there,
moves you up that line.
Do you have an honest report?

Are you full of wisdom,
full of the Holy Ghost?
He is the ingredient, you need the most.
That's bound to work.
Being filled with His Spirit will never hurt.
He is love, He is joy, sensitivity,
as He moves you on to maturity.

63

It Will Be Well

I did not dream a dream.
Nor did I see a scene.
But I tell you,
it will be well,
for I am a dreamer.
What I am coming to
is of the future do tell.
In the process of time
is not of my mind.
Our world will be confronted.
Not from a trance,
not of a vision,
do I tell what I see.
It's the Word speaking to me.
Our future is destined to be
packed with joy and harmony.
Don't take it from me—
check the Word and you will see
nothing but joy and harmony.
As I fasten my mind's eye on God's Word,
what liberty!
The flood of understanding
what our future will surely be.
I consider and see harmony
between God and the heart of man
through all our land.

As the Spirit bids you,
go with the Word.
Nothing doubting,
the Word touting.
Our future is destined to be
packed with joy and harmony.
Don't take it from me—
check the Word and you will see.
Nothing but joy and harmony.
Joy, joy, oh boy!
A source of pleasure or satisfaction
could lead to a state of relaxation.
Harmony, gee whiz,
a pleasant combination,
causing a whole,
where the church is heading, I'm told.
Our future is destined to be
packed with joy and harmony.
Don't take it from me—
check the Word and you will see.
Nothing but joy and harmony.
This joy of God, I do employ.
I will sing and dance because that is my choice.
The only one who can bring to a stop
this joy, you see, is me.
Having so much fun,
I may even run.
I can't opt out of this
joy, joy, joy.
I won't opt out.
Let's continue;
let's shout.

64

Recouped It All

When you were played for a fool,
they most certainly bent the rule.
If then they stretched the truth
into a lie, so very cruel.
If when all you own, they stole,
you can recoup it all;
the Word makes you bold.
There is no defeat
that is absolute and complete,
that cannot be reversed
and denied the right to repeat.

Check out the promises from your Father to you.
Every word is faithful.
Every word is true.
Believing what it said is your part,
blurting the words out
in faith from the heart.
Check out the promises from your Father to you.
That's the progression;
that is what you do.

Sometimes your health
may seemingly not be on par.
You know, it's a little like having
a secured door ajar.

Using the Word,
kick out what illegally came in,
after your repentance of any known sin.
Now, close that door,
sealing it with the Word galore,
all the Scriptures on healing
that you heard before.

Check out the promises from your Father to you.
Every word is faithful,
every word is true.
Believing what it said is your part,
blurting the words out,
in faith from the heart.
Check out the promises from your Father to you.
That's the progression.
That is what you do.

Recoup it all; recoup it all.
No matter the measure of the depth of the fall,
He will allow you to recoup it all.
Recoup it all; recoup it all.
No matter the reason or the cause of the fall,
He will allow you to recoup it all.

Check out the promises from your Father to you.
Every word is faithful,
Every word is true.
Believing what it said is your part,
blurting the words out,
in faith from the heart.

*Check out the promises from your Father to you,
that's the progression; that is what you do.*

Recoup it all; that's your part to play.
Don't you dare wait;
give in to no delay.

Recoup it all; recoup it all.
That's the Spirit-filled, on-fire
child of God's way.
Recoup it all.
The enemy's in shock.
You, he couldn't stop.
Can't figure how his defeat came about.
But we know that God
canceled him out.
Praise God, praise God—
we recouped it all.

The next composition speaks of a song I carried to India back in 2011. There, at the Bible school, I took the opportunity to introduce what I deemed to have been a blessing to our family. The students loved it. The following morning, I could hear the young men, as they took their showers, belting out the song. That brought tears to my eyes. For a long time following our return home, I received emails and texts from students inquiring, in one way or another, about that song. My desire is that this blesses you, as well.

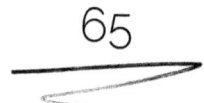

Good Morning, Jesus

While at Rhema—
back then "Rhema Bible Training School"—
we learned a song that was a jewel,
introduced by the dean,
so very supreme.
He planted what I believed
to have been a seed.
First thing,
in that room before class had begun,
that song was sung.
It became a tool for our family
and our ministry.
Through it, hearts were
and are increased.
You know, God uses that which is simple
to push through His agenda.

Well, nothing is as simple
as what you are about to hear,
but listen with your heart
and not just your ear.

Good morning, Jesus.
Good morning, love.
I know you are sent from heaven above.
The Holy Spirit descends on you like a dove.
Good morning, Jesus.
Good morning, Love.

In a couple of years,
when our first grandchild appeared,
she, we did not awake,
with a yell or a shake.
She, we did not awake,
with a loud
or a soft shout.
That song took precedence
as we sang in our residence,
introducing it to Chelsea,
singing softly in her ears,
the comforting lyrics, removing fears.
This was done
with one exception—
replacing her name in the song.
Believe you me, that was not disrespectful nor wrong,
but spiritually insightful was what I heard.
Then deep inside, my heart was stirred
as I began singing.

Good morning, Chelsea.
Good morning, Love.
I know you were sent from heaven above.
The Holy Spirit descends on you like a dove.
Good morning, Chelsea.
Good morning, Love.

And so it was with the remaining three, you see:
Good morning, Tristyn.
Good morning, Love.
Good morning, Jordyn.
Good morning, Love.
Good morning, Maxwell.
Good morning, Love.
I know you were sent from heaven above.
The Holy Spirit descends on you like a dove.
Good morning, Tristyn.
Good morning, Jordyn.
Good morning, Maxwell.
Good morning, Love.

Praise God, our grands
Have, for the most part,
matured and have offspring of their own,
blessing us with great-grands.
I tell you,
the great-grands are
high rates.
We are back singing the song again.
Good morning, Sophia.
Good morning, Love.
Good morning, Quest.

Good morning, Love.
I know you were sent from heaven above.
The Holy Spirit descends on you like a dove.
Good morning, Sophia.
Good morning, Love.
Good morning, Quest.
Good morning, Love.

Singing "Good Morning, Jesus" never did leave us.
In fact, the blessing of the Christmas meal
is always followed with that song,
blessed in that special way,
on that special day:
swapping out "good morning" for "happy birthday."
Happy birthday, Jesus.
Happy birthday, Love.
I know You are sent from heaven above.
The Holy Spirit descends on You like a dove.
Happy birthday, Jesus.
Happy birthday, Love.

Should God place on your heart to follow suit,
insert your loved one's name
there on their birthday
or give them a morning treat
to start the day off sweet.

66

Cities of Unrest

To the ones who blaspheme,
you need to fear
the words you hear.
God can send out a blast.
It can happen so fast
that you will dispute your very victory.
But refrain—check out the book.
It is recorded in so many places
how our God has fought for the righteous cause,
but you know not the manner of the land.
He has tempered justice from mercy.
But I promise this is not what you will see.
He will send rumors
that you will believe.
You will fall by the sword of your own hand
if your love is not restored to this land.

O! Portland, this is a word for you.
Kenosha, you will be exposed, too.
Lose your liberty in a huff.
You'll rebuff;
don't you fuss.
Refrain in Jesus' name.

There are cities of unrest in our nation,
pockets of ungodly authority.
Take note; this is a quote,
under political choke.
Oh me! Oh my!
That won't at all fly.
Understand this game,
in Jesus' name.

LA, you need to watch what you say.
Sign a bill
for man's will
to have sex with the undefiled.
That's a child,
age nine or ten;
this kind of sin
will do you in.
Your game is seen, in Jesus' name.

O Portland, another word for you:
Pull back from what you say.
Kick out the crud that's choking you.
They limit all the good you do.
Killing and stealing,
destroying all you were,
believing
is their only agenda, I say.
Civil help can come today,
but your leaders say, "No way.
"We can handle it;
we won't dismantle it,
for it fits into our narrative display."

Check the book out—it's recorded so many places.
Our God will fight for His righteous,
you see.
God will send out a blast.
It will happen so fast.
They will dispute our victory.
There are cities of unrest in our nation
with pockets of ungodly authority.

Oh me, oh my
That won't at all fly.

Take note:
Far too much is a hoax.
And me, you may quote.

67

Of Which We Are

God stands in the midst of the mighty,
of which we are,
of which we are by far.
He is leading the poor and fatherless.
Who, more times than not are profitless.
Justice gives He to the afflicted one.
He delivers the poor and needy son,
ridding him of the wicked one.
Often before the day is done.

Arise, God, and judge the earth,
for You will inherit all nations,
filling me with expectations.
God stands in the midst of the mighty,
and it matters not who they all might be
of which we are,
of which we are by far.
The lion has roared.
Who will not fear?
With or without a tear,
It is so very clear.
The Lord our God has spoken.

68

O Isles

Listen, O isles, unto me.
Give attention, you people, from afar.
I bring you the word,
which from God have I heard.
How His Son did die for the cause.

Oh! How they hit, and they spit.
They betrayed;
they did degrade.
They did lie, for Him to die.
He refused;
He would not choose
to abandon the plan.
In the grave three days
is how He paid.
For you and for me,
He could not see
giving up on Calvary.

He did it all- that we would not fall.
Though Satan tried his very best,
Jesus followed through on His Father's behest.
Listen, O isles, unto me.

Give attention, you people, from afar,
there beyond the sea
I bring you the word
that from God have I heard,
how His Son did die for your cause.
He would have done it
had you been the only one.
He would have died,
the Father's only Son.
For together, they did agree—
the Father, Son, Spirit—the three.
So, listen, O isles, unto me.

69
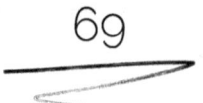

Political Atmosphere

Thank You, Father for Your rhythm,
during our nation's greatest time of derision.
Those who hate us, see us as a laughingstock,
Constantly laughing and oh how they do mock.

An object of ridicule, they are so very cruel.
Some say we have become derelict
and worthy to be kept behind
in the world's race and conflict.
They have thought us to be neglectful
in duty and obligation.
But You, Lord, did not abandon this massive operation.
You labeled us worthy, as in dignity.
Lord, Your movements were surely marked
as regular occurrences,
and often resurgences sparked,
with a tinge of different conditions and durations.
Your way for a better day
was meted out without a doubt,
constructed by You, as if by measure.
As the Word did relate,
it all had to be by faith,
doled out through Your entire body,
of which we are.
Thank God we are looking at this from our view.

What a venue,
an absolute expansive location of crime
based on our political atmosphere:
So broad, so wide . . .
So deep, so near . . .
No jury to call,
no trial to be had,
before derision set in and our enemies were mad.
And I am not using that word in the context of anger.

No, they had to be inflicted with a mental disorder,
displaying furious intensity,
believe you me.
All in an attempt to help the masses see
the truth of what evil brought to our nation,
almost canceling our liberty.
But now—now we are back on track.
Well, not quite right.
My oversight!
We are much better than that,
as we are MAGA,
thanking our ABBA.
We all answered that call.
We who?
We who are of Him
and who know His Word.
We all should have answered that call
to make America great again.
That call should have been answered by all.

70

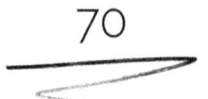

We Bow to the Bid

It all must bow
at Your bidding.
As with a suave auctioneer,
it all must be acknowledged
when spoken clear.
Not that incoherent jargon,
concerning a worthless bargain.
Every brain cell comes to attention,
with the posture to accept what you mention
of the Word only
and that testimony.
Although the enemy says you are poor and sick,
defeated, depressed,
as if your life is on an auction block,
he is a liar—you are not in a lock.
Every fiber in you
waits your rebuke,
so they can bow unto you.
This is not a fluke.
Go ahead say, "Be still,
"I'm healed."
You say,
"I have the victory."
You say, "You'll see,
"I offer that decree."

So, they can bow to the bid of your dictate.
No other terms need you relay.
You have won.
You have won this battle,
no matter.
And it matters not, today, what anyone else may say.

71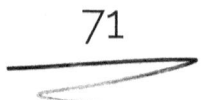

Oh, How I've Changed

You have certainly worked on me.
I look now always for victory.
What a change.
There's a change in my attitude.
That's a change in my brain.
I came to this point
by acknowledging Jesus' reign.

When bodily attitude is set
in an awkward position.
When it depicts
a different coalition.
When it shows to others a default,
just by the way I carry myself,
to them that is my fault.
That, too, has been rearranged.
What a change.

There's a change in my fortitude.
That's a change in my strength,
affording power of mind,
allowing me to endure,
absolutely for sure.
I endure adversity courageously,
although sometimes through the pain,
the hardship does remain.
But still, what a change.

There's a change in how I perceive,
as in becoming aware of initially.
It is processed through the senses,
that is the soul,
I am told, you see,
the storehouse for all my rememberings.
New insight made right,
day or night.
The Word I speak comes from my spirit
to that soul
for absolute control.
Sparking a change, it could be just a suggestion
for godly acceptance.
What a change.

There's a change in how I think,
that is, every issue out.
I reason about, without doubt.
I reflect on what I must decide.
That helps me to abide.
Thinking simply means to remember.
Very innocent from that perspective to either gender,
but then the definition degenerates from there.
Starting with mental preoccupation,
it could be the precursor to life's damnation.
How about an example of thinking self into a panic?
Maybe to you "I" seem a bit maverick.
And then, of course, they must go from there to here.
An antidote for fear,
they say,
"is to exercise the power of reason."
After having left God out?

I say not, not in this nor any other season.
The last three you can see,
you, it will absolutely freeze,
and bring you to your knees.
Allow no thought to occupy you
that you need not ever do.
Whatever you are thinking about,
bow out
before panic attacks
and stops you in your tracks.
Always remember, the "reason" we overcome
is because of the power of the Son.
Not the "power of reason,"
no matter the season.

72

Spirit of All Ages

Completed February 15, 2024

The Spirit of all ages
wants to speak to you
from those pages.
But given the due, respect due,
What will you do?
Will you lend your ear to?

He is able to perform your need,
unquestionably indeed.
Now, to understand what it is all about,
please check this out.
In John's connoting of what Jesus said,
That, I've already read.
Past tense, I have already seen.
Do you know what I mean?
There in verse thirteen of chapter sixteen,
to be not stuck,
look it up.
When He, the Spirit of truth, has come,
He will impart the total sum.
All truth He will guide you into
by taking what is mine and showing it unto you.
That He will do.
All things the Father has,

Jesus said, "are Mine."
Implementing the possibility
of those things becoming thine.
We must not be tenuous concerning this issue,
being firmly grounded in this venue is
my desire for you.
Now, please listen to this important clue.

And be confident, as well, these are revelations,
coming from the God of all nations.

The chain of command was established by Him.
The chain of command was established by them.
Just as when God said in Genesis one and twenty-seven,
we must throw this in, as it came right out of Heaven-

"Let us make man in our image."
In the image of God,
created He him.
Male and female,
created He them.
So, if the He who speaks in Genesis
is, indeed, the same,
He, in John, where He said,
and I know you remember what we read;
"The Spirit will not speak *only* of Himself,"
then the Spirit will not speak *lonely* of Himself.
"Whatever the Spirit will hear from us"
(spoken by the Father and the Son),
The Spirit will show you those things to come.

I do believe we have a solid platform,
from which to roam.
The Bible is a document. And it will always complement.
It supports itself with references, addressing our differences
backed by records birthed in antiquity,
the gathering and coding of printed materials
for future actualities,
confirming our rights to be free
from confinement, servitude, forced labor,
and governmental control,
all of which pressures our soul.

You may ask, "How is this done?"
Only by the power of the Father, the Spirit, and the Son.

Keep your spiritual eyes open.
Remember, His job is to show you things to come.
There should be nothing to slip up on you unaware.
The Father and Son gave the Spirit to us for our care.
Yes, this is a solid platform
with much room to roam.
I believe I have conveyed a valid
an imaginative sense of this- And if not, then what did I miss?
This may not necessarily be a poem, or a prose, but a composition
and that is how it goes.

Now, let me direct you back to the premise,
where the subject is generis.
Merely because the
Bible is unique and highly peculiar,
as it helps us to escape failure.
Nothing here delusional.

Well, here we are for the last time,
the statement, quite sublime.

The Spirit of all ages
wants to speak to you from those pages.
But given the due,
respect due, you.
 Will you allow Him to?

73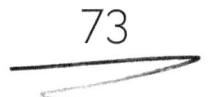

I Must Chant

It all belongs to You, God, and not me.
For You made all of what I now see.
Even the battle belongs to You, Lord.
Yes, the battle belongs to You.

As with Judah, to the sound of Your music
I must chant.
You see, I have no right to rant,
so I'll just chant.

As You send forth Your angels to prosper my way,
every moment of time of every day.
Deep inside me,
my spirit will agree.
I have a God-given right to be free.
This, I promise,
and do it, I will.
I will chill.
No right to rant,
I will chant.

I will take my place in the battle.
I will keep my place in You, Lord.
I will not break rank.
Such an evil prank.
No right to rant.
I will chant.
I must chant to the sound of Your music,
with a sense of the therapeutic.

74

Finding Grace

All my acts, ways, and conflicts too
are laid before my Lord
as if He did record.
Not, though,
but seemingly so.

His hand remains stretched out still.
My number-one desire is to do His will.
We all need noise about how He is in our heart.
His presence is always with us,
not ever just in part.
He gives us constant rest,
as He is always the same.
Jesus made it so
that we find grace in His name.

75

Innocent Blood

*B*ound and led away,
my Savior was on that day.
Stood before Pilate, they say.

Judas, who betrayed Him,
heard them condemn Him.

Then claimed he,
"Innocent blood was betrayed by me."
Stated, "innocent blood."
Asserted, "innocent blood."
Is still claiming, "innocent blood".
It will always be innocent blood.
For eternity, innocent blood,
He gave for you and me,
on that chosen tree,
innocent blood.
It was required.
Innocent blood was demanded.
So, the Son of God was handed.

Oh, that blood of Jesus—
there is something about that innocent blood,
how it flowed like a flood.
Even now, all led astray
can claim, this day,
innocent blood.

76

Trees of the Field

The trees of the field know He is God.
He brought down the high tree.
Exalted the low tree.
Dried up the green tree.
Flourished the dry tree.
A demonstration of victory,
I guarantee.
He, the Lord, spoke it.
He, the Lord God, did it,
and He needed no permit.

If it had not been for the Lord,
who was on our side,
when they revolted against us,
tried to quickly consume us,
seething all around us,
filled with cuss and discuss,
there would have been no one else to trust.

Blessed be the Lord,
Who gave us not as prey of defeat.
As a bird from the snare of the fowler,
our soul did not retreat.
The trap was broken, and we escaped.
Our help is in the name of the Lord.
Against that, there is no debate.

He made heaven and earth,
Adam, Eve, and that includes the ones
to whom she gave birth.

He has done all things well,
making the deaf to hear
the word of the Lord;
making the dumb to speak
the word of the Lord and fear;
making the blind to see
the word of the Lord with victory;
making the lame to walk.
What great exalt,
the word of the Lord will impart.

77

Wield the Word

The supply for the crisis has already been made.
The means by which we secure it is already paid.
It all depends upon us.
On us it will depend,
from the beginning to the end.
We will eat the fruit of our doings,
if in the past, we planted.
Then what we do,
what we say,
can shift the blessings our way.
Say, ask, demand
that the supply be at hand;
that your manifestation,
the simplest of our part,
be that of our heart.
I say to the righteous,
"It shall be well.
"If your heart does not waver,
"you will eat the fruit of your labor,
"packed, with savor.
"Have refuge from heat and cold.
"Take refuge from storms and their toll.
"So go ahead, wield the Word of the Lord,
"like a sword."

78

Battle

I will take my place in the battle
I will keep my place in You, Lord.
I will not break rank,
for there is no metal of thanks,
when I break rank.

The battle belongs to You, Lord.
You made what I see.
You gave it to me.
I will give You due respect.
Nothing about You
will I ever reject.
You made it, then You gave it.
We lost it.
So You brought it back.
None can argue.
That's a given fact.

All that You gave, which was lost,
was brought back at the highest cost.

Oh! But You know the one who stole it
 will come again and again for it.
So, You left not the plan
in the hand
of no other,
outside of the Son of Man.

79

Speak His Name

"We have been with Jesus,"
is what the disciples said.
I know this because
that is what I read.
This, you may already know:
How that, the boldness in them did show.
A notable miracle had been done.
No one could deny.
Don't waste your time,
Don't even try.

Rumors were spreading ahead,
among the townspeople.
Now, some said what they had done
was not legal.
So, they tried to shut the talk down,
all around town.
The threat of censoring will subside.
With God we will abide.
That is what they did prophesy.
To command us to not speak is weak.
Demanding we not teach
in Jesus' name? How freak.
His character, His purpose, we must expose:
how He died and how He rose.

It is not right in God's sight
to hearken to you,
day or night.
We cannot but speak His name.
The things which we have seen and heard,
we proclaim.

His name is Jesus, —
Jesus, my Lord,
the mighty King,
Master of everything.
All who see, glorify God
when a miracle is done
through His Son.

Great grace is upon each one.
Great grace is upon you.
Great grace is upon you, too.
Great grace is upon you, and
you and you.

80

Reservoir for My Ministry

Thank You for Your Word, Lord.
Your Word I have heard.
It has now become a reservoir for my ministry.
A lamp unto my feet
it continues to be.
Unto my paths,
the light shines, never ceasing,
never ever decreasing.

Thank You, Lord, for the Word heard
perpetually being, eternally streaming,
forever being a reservoir for ministry.

For hours, days, years to come,
by that same word, they will be won.
In my future,
even into eternity,
I have a reservoir for ministry.

So, I go into Your Word, Lord.
I'm going in.
You see me going in,
perpetual streaming,
eternally being.

For hours, days, years to come,
not my will, but Yours be done.
This Word, Lord,
will be spoken.
That promise to You,
will not be broken.

You have given me, so freely,
Time for this opportunity.
I deny not Your quest
to bring to this world Your very best.
After having gone into Your Word,
It is always You that I have heard.
You see me going in,
long before I even begin

Your Word, unto my feet,
a lamp, continuing to be,
never ceasing.
And for me not ever decreasing.
The light that You shine unto my path,
Is eternally being and
perpetually streaming.
It is a reservoir for ministering
to those in the path of my future.
Yes, what You will say I will do Sir.
For hours, days, years to come,
Your call to me, Lord, will be done.
So, I go into Your Word, Lord.
Now, I'm going in.
This call has a beginning,
but I honestly see no end.

I'll be established,
in every good word,
and every good work.
Nothing there to ever hurt.

Here I am, inquiring at the Word of the Lord today.
I'm looking for light for the future, per se.
What God tells me,
that and only that will I do,
allowing the light of the Word,
to flow on through.

81
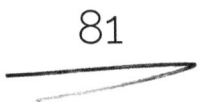

The Worth of What Is Missing

Have you ever had a loved one to steal from you?
And if so, what on God's green earth did you do?
Maybe you took precautions, not to believe.
May I now ask, just who was deceived?
By not providing them with an opportunity to deny,
their conscience you did satisfy.
Where there is adequate evidence,
you must allow them the opportunity
to set their defense.
Firstly, access the mess,
for it is truly a test.
And, you must strive to do your best,
leaving for God the rest.
All of what you are faced with,
is not yours to attend.
Amen?
Yours to do, or undo,
you cannot do that which
God has not assigned to you.
Get out of God's way.
Only your part play.
Should you not hearken,
brace for a great delay,
of God's predestined array,
of glory, which should have come your way.

Now you know
that loved one is worth far more
than the worth of what is missing.
And there is a good chance
the culmination of the issue
very soon will be brought to fruition.

82

Solid Rock

As the suave auctioneer acknowledges the bid,
I give Christ the glory, acknowledging what He did.
Every brain cell surrenders and bows, my Lord,
before You,
and that they will always do
with a not-so-visible salute.
But a very prescribed justice
kicked in because He fetched us.
Lord, it all must bow at Your bidding.
It may seem to many
that my life is on the auction block.
But I don't believe such a thought,
for I'm on the Solid Rock.

I know the enemy says that I am poor.
I know the enemy says that I am always sick.
The enemy says that defeat is mine
all the time.
The enemy says, "depressed" with all the rest,
as if my life is on the auction block.
I will say it again:
On the Solid Rock I stand.

My every brain cell surrenders and bows before You;
That, they will always do.
You said, "Be still."
You said, "Be healed."
You said to me, "Victory."
You said, "Rejoice and see."
So, I bow to the bid of Your offered decree.
I have already won.
My victory, Christ has done.
I have already won.
Ha! Ha!
It's done.
I have already won.
I have already won.
Ha! Ha!
It's done.
I have already won—
all thanks to the Son.

83

Sing from the Heart

Let nothing take a song
with the Word of God in it
out of your heart.
Do your part.
Sing from the heart.

Softly singing or maybe even belting
from beginning to ending.
That is your part.
Sing from the heart.
Your praise will raise,
the ceiling for your healing.

When your balance for walking has eluded you,
prancing and dancing
is soon what you'll do.
For your praise will raise
the ceiling for your healing.

I am not doubting
that at the moment
your body's not functioning quite right.
But you do have a just,
loyal title or claim to walk, or run, tonight.
If you feel a skip coming on,
you can do that, too.

An action so powerful,
why would you then not do?
Get this visual of yourself:
Slide, glide, from the left to the right side.
You are not ashamed,
with nothing to hide,
so, slide then glide.
Come on, ride this thought out
to victory,
firmly planted in belief.
If healing is, indeed, the children's bread,
and that is what I have always read.
Then the digesting of the Scripture,
along that category,
will surely afford the desired glory.
There will be no reflux to upchuck,
Because all that Word you do need.
There is not a part that is not your seed.
Proclaim it again and again
until you keep it in,
saying, "by His stripes I am healed,
even though the pain I can feel.
He bore my sin,
and He bore my pain
on a tree,
so that all would be well with me.
He was wounded for my transgressions, you see.
I don't have to be".
Wounded, that is.
Glory!
He was also bruised for my iniquity.
The chastisement of my peace was laid upon Him.

By His stripes, healed I have been.
I just got that understanding.
Revelation at last, at last, at last.
The Word, I confess
to ward off attacks on my wellness.

Why wait until a symptom pops up?
My head is anointed with oil,
and running over is my cup.
Yes, it is sealed that I am healed.

84

I Vow

I sense down the line in time,
there will be no stiffening of my neck,
no blame or reproach on which to reflect.
I vow, no hardening of the heart,
to abort.
There will be no occasion to say, "Woe is me now."
To what You have planned, for my life, I vow.
I will always find rest,
and profess, I will not transgress.

Although there will be occasions to turn foul,
times like that I will most certainly disavow.
For all that I plant,
my desire is that none be plucked up,
and full and running over will be my cup.

I thank you all from deep, deep within—
my father, my brother, my friend.
I am seeking only great things for my life,
for me, there will be no evil outpouring of strife.
I am Your very own dwelling place,
and the world is our massive showcase.
I am in You.

You live in me
forever and ever,
to be removed, never—
not ever.
I will not be confounded and taken.
I will not be dismayed when mistakes are mistaken
No "sad story for me ", displayed.
My victories will not be delayed.
Oh, Lord, the way I should go
was never in me to know.
For it is not in the one walking
to direct their own steps.
As our life's journey is often stressed
Why take on that chore
when it has never worked before?
Living is packed with trying,
but Your Word I will be applying.
I avow, dear Lord,
that down the line in time,
my life will be prime and sublime.

Fashioned by the word,
by Your design.
So, I thank You from deep, deep within.
Yes, I say to You, my dear friend.
Thank you, thank you again.

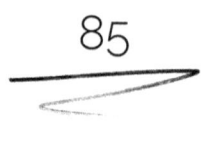

We Win

*S*hedding tears upon my pillow is the least I can do.
Offering prayers to our God concerning you—
that I do, too.
Words of protection,
words of reflection,
reminding Him of who you are,
and what you do.
Maybe even sharing how He
has always brought you through,
matters not the test,
the degree, the length, and all the rest.
You win, you win again.
You yell it out as loud as you can:
"I win, I win again."
There is strength in numbers, I will admit.
So, let's just, together, stick.
We will show love to one another,
by supporting each other.
No matter the test,
the degree, the length, all the rest,
I win, I win—amen!

He saves us from all who persecute us.
He delivers us from the rising of the sun to dusk.
The wickedness of the wicked
will come to an end,
but as for us, our God will defend.
Establishing the just,
the pillars of heaven,
as they are leavened,
tremble and are astonished at His reproof.
He divides the sea with power.
The proud He plunders through.
But we win—we win again.

86

To Do Your Will

I am grateful, Father, for Your Word,
the only picture I have ever heard.
Sketching the scheme of my future, both near and far,
only to reflect the image of who You are.
Thank You, Father, for Your Word,
the most comforting sound I have ever heard,
drumming out encouragements of life's future,
for God's achievers not worldly losers,
for daily, weekly, yearly events,
as the occasion always presents.

As I wrap my mind around what You do,
sometimes
remembering back before even knowing You.
But I stand alone,
in that thought.
For, never a time was I not in Your heart.

When was it You did not view me?
When was it You did not love me?
When was it You did not choose me
to do Your will?

When was it You did not prep me?
When was it You did not prepare me?
When was it You did not purpose me
to do Your will?

I am exultant, Father, for Your Word,
as said before, "the only picture I have ever heard.
exciting flow of times and happenings on verge?
Not stuck in decades of stifling,
but cuddled as You shuffled me in,
causing me to give up on that sin.
I have pleasure, Father, with Your Word,
again, the only picture I have ever heard.
That epic enjoyment from Your inner most part
freely flowing, freely taught,
from You to me divinely.

As I wrap my mind around what You do,
sometimes remembering back before even knowing You.
But I stand alone in that thought.
There was never a time I was not in Your heart.
And so, it is with the reader,
for they too are a significant part.

When was it He did not view you?
When was it He did not love you?
When was it He did not choose you,
to do His will?
When was it He did not prep you?
When was it He did not prepare you?
When was it He did not purpose You
to do His will?
So, we stand, O God in Your presence still,
To do your word,
exactly as heard.

87

We Thank You

We thank You and praise You, too, for all that You are.
We thank You and praise You, too,
for what we have thus far.
For all You have given us,
thank You we must.
For our children, which You have graciously loaned,
we know they are ours;
we know they are owned.
But as if uncontrollably driven,
daily we thank You,
for how they were given.
There are no means by which to compensate You
for whom You are and for all that You do.
So sometimes we groan within, as in pain.
The pressure of our gratitude remains and remains.
Then we must remove that cap,
and let the sound out.
At the top of our voice, we shout,
"Ooh, ooh, ooh.
"LORD, I LOVE YOU."
As the ancestors did back in history,
that, too, tells His-story, not always with words,
sometimes just an utter.
Still, You give attention
to that babble and mutter.

To others, it is low and indistinctly spoken,
but to You, an indication
or representation of emotion.
So, we groan and moan,
though the sound is not clear.
Dear God, my Lord, we know that You hear.
We thank You
and praise You, too,
for all that You are.
We thank You and praise You, too,
for what we have thus far.
For all You have given us,
thank You, we must.
We thank You
and praise You, too,
for Your generous trust.

88

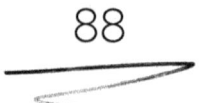

Your Now Is Yours

Your now is yours to do.
With it,
what you do is yours, too.
Tomorrow is not promised to you,
so do all you can do,
before the day is done.
Let it not be said you helped no one.
Your now is yours to do.

As the sun descends,
this day ends.
I've been protected once again.
Hidden in His glory
will always be my story
of how the next day began
and how that day will end.

The hours come.
The hours go.
Never a struggle—
watch them flow.
From morning to night, the only change
is how I use the time that remains.

Your now is yours to do.
With it,
what you do is yours, too.
Tomorrow is not promised to you.
So, do all you can do
before the day is done.
Let it not be said
that you helped no one.
Your now is yours to do.

Some days, more than others, are eventful.
Some are good, some bad and resentful.
No matter the day
you are faced with now,
help comes from the One to whom you bow.
He is always available
to provide you with care.
He will protect,
as He is always there.

Your now is yours to do.
With it,
what you do is yours, too.
Time can't ever be reclaimed—
not a moment,
not a minute,
not an hour—
no matter your level of power.
Not a day,
not a week,
not a month,
certainly not a year.

Time is not yours.
Do you hear?
Hear me now—don't forget.
Do good that you'll never regret.
Hear me now—don't forget.
Doing good will benefit.
Hear me now—don't forget.
Your now is yours to do.
But you must choose to.

Flows My Portion

His blood is upon the door seal of my family bloodline.
We live a quiet, peaceable life,
in the midst of that strife.
No matter how things soar,
it will not affect us in any way for sure.
We know how to have His Kingdom come.
His Word we use to get it done.

I'm in a land greater than the land of Goshen,
for where I am daily, hourly, flows my portion.
Whatever my need,
I look to my seed.
When it's buried deeply
and fertilized,
I sprinkle gently to waterize.
His Word I use to get that done.
The quickest way to have His Kingdom come.
For the Lord our God has persevered
throughout all the earth,
our posterity from birth.
Our entire future is saved by His great deliverance.
We'll not be overcome
by any hindrance.

His blood is upon the door, the seal of my family bloodline.
So, we live a quiet, peaceable life in the midst of that strife.
It matters not how you see,
our future will be.
You were not the one who granted our liberty.
Why would I be so foolish to consider words of poverty?
You'll not speak that degradation over me.

I'm in a land greater than the land of Goshen,
for where I am daily, hourly, flows my portion.
Whatever my need,
I look to my seed.
When it's buried deeply and fertilized,
I sprinkle it gently to waterize.
His words I use to get that done.
The quickest way to have His Kingdom come.
Wherever we are, our God does nourish.
Everything we touch will blossom and flourish.

Let me share with you the glory behind our door.
How the Word supplies our need,
as it has done so often before,
time and time and time again, and it always will.
The promises are ours to have—He will fulfill.
His blood is upon the door, the seal of my family bloodline.
So, we live a quiet, peaceable life in the midst of that strife.
No matter how things soar,
outside our door,
it will not affect us in any way for sure.
We know how to have His Kingdom come.
His Word we use to get it done.

Another word of encouragement and guarantee:
Give respect to all placed by God in authority.
Praying for them is only God's reality,
in all godliness and honesty.
This is good and acceptable
in the sight of God, our Savior.
He wills all to come into His knowledge, truth, and favor.

We're in a land greater than
the land of Goshen,
for where we are flows daily, hourly,
our portion.

90

You Aren't Wearing That

You are not going to wear that anytime soon.
Not morning, not nighttime, for sure not at noon.
I love it when Mommy helps me dress.
One time sticks out, I must confess.
Mommy said, way back in June,
"You are not wearing that anytime soon."
At the time, I was sad.
Kinda made me mad.
But around Mommy, I forced looking glad.
Now, months later, I'll not forget, nor let it slip,
how she stood there looking at me,
with her hand on her hip.
Then Mommy said,
"Clothing is personal, and desires are, too,
"but you are not going to wear that anytime soon.
"With that factual statement I just made to you,
"there could be limitations, such as playacting at school.
"Or even at home, using your imagination,
"with no realization.
"But you will have learned
"to separate in your heart
"the real from the fake;
"Pull it apart.

"No, you are not going to wear that anytime soon.
"Not morning, not nighttime, for sure not at noon.
"Certain styles are not for you,
"clothes or shoes,
"but you will learn to coordinate
"before it is too late."
Know that dressing modestly is in,
though maybe not with your closest friend.
The right thing to do is always stay on God's side.
In the future, you will be okay with nothing to hide,
void of that pride.
This premise needs emphasis.
I think it is very wise.

You are not going to wear that anytime soon.
Now, when you're older, you will decide certain things to do, never.
And with Jesus and me, this practice remains the same,
yesterday, today, and forever.

91

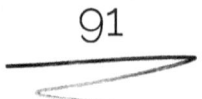

Conversion from Perversion

I thank God we did see with our eyes.
With our ears we did hear.
We understood with our heart
the essential part.

That's conversion from perversion.
As a nation, let's get back to what is normally
right.
Power to corrupt, misuse, misconstrue will be removed,
will not be legally used.
Suddenly we will be able to make that decision,
supplied by God's Word with all provision.
We are not in this alone,
even to some worldly, that is known.
As if blindly, we tread,
being without sight,
not knowing what's right.
But we see with our eyes.
With our ears we do hear.
We understand with our heart,
the essential part.

Should you no longer believe
this United States to be a godly nation,
with its "cancel culture,"
identity crises, and border invasion,
I tell you; mankind will never be the one to draw the line.
This country remains as it was in previous time:
God reserved.
God preserved.
God deserved.
This country can always be His.
Men, women traveling to other nations,
doing what God said.
saying what they have read,
in the hope our world would conform to God's thoughts,
understanding what His Son, Jesus, has brought.
Then trusting in Him despite consequences,
using the Word for all future defenses.
Jesus, You showed forth all long-suffering for a pattern
that we, who would come after, would use in any matter.
It is now that we are persuaded
that neither death, nor life,
will ever be able to separate us
from the love of Christ.

Because we see with our eyes.
With our ears we do hear.
We understand with our heart, the essential part.
That's conversion from perversion.
We are saved.
Thank You, Lord.
We are saved.

92
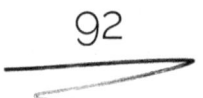

The Highway of the Upright

The preparation of man's heart—
the whole, not just part—
and the answer of the tongue, is from the Lord
when it's rightly done.
All the ways of man are clean in his own eyes,
but the Lord weighs the attitude, no matter the disguise.
Commit your works unto the Lord,
and your thoughts will be established.
You'll see decrease,
not increase, in those annoying old habits.
Our Lord has made all things for Himself.
Even evil He'll release,
and yes, an actively bad person
could be freed from their leash.
That won't shake me at all,
and neither am I appalled,
because my ways please.
He makes even my enemies
be at peace with me,
you see.

And this is the Word of the Lord to you.
He makes your enemies at peace with you, too.
Your heart will devise your ways,
but let the Lord direct your steps.
Take the highway of the upright.
That will be your great escape.
When you handle a matter wisely,
you will find God in it.
To you, it should not be surprisingly.

Trusting in the Lord will make you happy, as it should,
for your own good.

Pleasant words are as honeycomb,
sweet to the soul and healthy to the bone.
There is a way
that seems so right,
but at its finality, it can end your life.
And this is the Word of the Lord to you.
That way that seems so, right?
It doesn't have to end your life.
Your heart will devise your ways,
but let the Lord direct your steps.
Take the highway of the upright.
That is your escape.
It's the highway or no way.
Can you say, "Hooray"?
It is the highway or no way.
Hooray, hooray.

93

One Mountain

*S*peak to one mountain.
Believe it to be gone.
Don't try conquering it, for you would be wrong.
Just speak to that thing.
Believe it to be gone.

What is a mountain,
but a natural elevation of the earth's surface?
Nothing strange.
Nothing deranged.
It is not from another planet somewhere.
it is from here,
not from out there.
It's fixed right here, where it ought to be.
But then there's another mountain,
one you may not want to climb, but decree,
enforcing the proclamation of victory.
No going up one side, to descend with a stride.
Remove that thing from your life's test.
Saying what the Word says is always best.
Speak to that mountain—believe it to be gone.
That's how to conquer when for you it is wrong.
Speak to that thing.
Believe it to be gone.

You know I'm not talking about that object quite larger than a hill.
Attack the issue that's mocking you still.
Then watch it bow to your will.
Speak to *that* mountain; believe *it* to be gone.

94

I Look

I sure don't need evidence of You, O God.
It is all in my face, nothing there odd.
I look over here, and what do I see?
That great big, flourishing, fruit-filled tree.
Then I look over there,
and what do I hear?
The chirping of a feathered friend,
so melodically clear.
When I look down the hill
from where I stand,
I enjoy the flow of the water from land to land.
Now I tilt my head back as far as I can
and take in the untold vastness of the planetary,
God's spoken decree.
Now, if that's not enough, I'll give you another.
How about that out-of-body experience of the child
from the mother?
Evidence of You, O God, on the highest level.
But when it is sucked out and killed that's the devil!
I will not fret because of evildoers,
nor be envious of the iniquity pursuer.
It is the meek who will, indeed, inherit this earth,
and we will continue to delight ourselves in birth after birth after birth.

95

The Vault of Heaven

Though the heavens score the glory to God,
the totality of its fill will never be numbered.
The open expanse where birds fly is clearly our atmosphere.
But there is a space way out there, not at all near,
displaying the stars, the sun, the moon,
daily, nightly, so very soon.
But there is so much more that is there.
God's demonstration of love:
The vault of heaven, referred to as the arch above.
Space is broad, not limited at all,
except in the mind of man due to the Fall.
It is open for your view,
whatever there is to be seen by you.
Although we are now able to observe
all that our God did preserve,
that may not return until the lifetime of another.
But you will have been blessed,
even I must confess.

96

Commanded Blessing

Regarding all enemies of my estate,
God's promises to me are great.
Although they may come against me one way,
seven ways they will flee, this day I say.

The Lord has commanded the blessing,
but I must do the possessing
of all that I set my hand to do.
He has blessed me in the place
He has sent me unto.

I proclaim I will lend.
I will not borrow.
Neither will I be overwhelmed
by pain and horror.
I am never the tail.
The head I will always be,
perpetually above, never, ever beneath.
Should you want to know
how I continue in this flow,
I simply hearken unto the commandments of my God,
whom you can also know.

97

Send Him On

I 've seen the adversary.
I know his moves.
He's been at it for some time—
quiet, often smooth.
However, there is one of many things he can't do,
and that is to stay hidden from our view.
Eventually he will overplay his hand,
making it easy to identify this so-called man.
So then, I send him on, you see.
He's not coming in here, pointing his finger at me.
That's what I mean.
He's not coming in here,
pointing his finger at me.

I see him out there, doing this or that.
I'm keeping him on that same old track.
First, he comes to cast some doubt.
It doesn't take much to figure that out.
Next, he tries to seed what he believes.
Being smarter than him,
that I will never receive
So then, I send him on, you see,
because he's not coming in here,
pointing his finger at me.
That's what I mean.
He's not coming in here,
pointing his finger at me.

He who is working from the same old label
won't prop his slue foot under my table,
trying to be a friend to me
when I know he is my greatest enemy.
So, I send him on, you see.
He's not coming in here,
pointing his finger at me.
That's what I mean:
he's not coming in here,
pointing his finger at me.

Over, and over, and over again,
he steals the store.
But God gives more.
Over, and over, and over again,
when he pretends,
God will revenge.
Over, and over, and over again,
if he says this,
God says he missed.
Over, and over, and over again,
when he does this,
God removes that.
It's a spiritual fact.
The devil's been smacked,
heartily and noisily,
so don't be deceived,
heartily and noisily.
So, I send him on, you see.

He's not coming in here,
pointing his finger at me.
Do you agree?
He's not coming in here,
pointing his finger at me.
Now, what is it that causes him to get up and leave?
Only the Word you have heard and believe.
But you must speak it out of your mouth,
not run it around in your head,
as if scared.
Yell it loud,
as if in a crowd.

You're not coming in here,
pointing your finger at me.
Now he believes.
He's not in here,
pointing his finger at me.

98

I Have the Remedy

You're living with an attitude.
You're living with an attitude.
You've got a frown on your face,
and a slur in your mouth.
I have no idea what that's all about.

From you to me,
no due consideration.
When long ago, we started this buddy relation.
I can't even remember not knowing you.
To each other,
we've always been faithful and true.
But now you're living with an attitude.
Why are you being so crude?
Living with that attitude.

Every day, with me, you're short and rude,
cause you're living with an attitude.
To get over this stomp,
I must show your posture,
or otherwise, it'll surely cost ya.
Even though you speak indistinctly,
somehow, I get the drift.
It's slightingly.
To others, you have smeared my reputation,
giving a false illumination.

Oh, they don't really believe what you say.
They have noticed a change from day to day.
They, too, know you are living with an attitude.
Every day with me, you are short and rude,
because you're living with an attitude.

I have the remedy
to reclaim your identity.
The Word of God revealed to me.
You can find it in Acts two and four.
The Holy Ghost will help you shut that door.
Be filled with the Spirit,
and speak in tongues,
as the Spirit gives the utterance.
If you really want to live your life right,
He will empower you, day or night.
Don't be living with an attitude.
How crude and rude.

You can't change you.
You need His help,
for a long time now, I've felt.
When His power enters you,
then you'll see you, too,
and you'll know just what to do,
empowered to change that attitude,
never again to be fooled.
You can change that attitude,
entering a pleasant aptitude.
I tell you,
you can change that attitude,
very soon.

99

Lift Up Your Eyes and Look

It's all there in God's Book.
Lift your eyes and look.
How else can you see intellectually
unless you inspect and regard what you now see?
It's been set in stone how I will be.
We must live to see and employ
the experience we now enjoy,
which was cloaked in the secrecy
of God's hidden command and decree.
It's revealed, no more sealed.
What was sealed is now revealed.
Though so near it was not clear,
but now, thank God, it's here.
Lift your eyes and look.
It's all there in God's Book.
There is understanding we will gain
that determines the level of our reign.
His desire is that we ascertain
all lost in the Garden that we can reclaim.
So be fully aware, with a position of trust.
He only trust, as He is just.

It's revealed, no more sealed,
What was sealed is now revealed.
Though so near it was not clear,
but now, thank God, it's here.
The Father, the Son I imitate.
The Spirit helps me to relate.
To communicate with God,
as the prophets we know not how,
but the means by which revelation appeared
is not as great as what we have now.
Our covenant better; the promises, too.
The knowledge we gain is binding and true.
It's revealed, no more sealed.
What was sealed
is now revealed.
Though it was so near, it was not clear.
But now, thank God, it's here.
What is here that is now clear?
Salvation, that is so real.

100

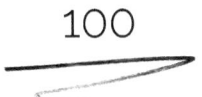

How Would You Be Rated?

The ability to make a decision,
the ability to form an opinion,
must be discerned and evaluated.
Not rushed through, but belated.

Snapping back through the fingers, inflicting pain,
envision that piece of elastic,
much like a word in the wrong season,
most assuredly perceived sarcastic.
That, too, is as much a spillage
as a caustic liquid can be sharp and bitter,
burning to the heart,
giving an immediate spark.
Although it is the right word, it must agree with time.
From you to them,
be it she or him.
The first to be considered must be time.
Don't expect success
should you kick this bucket down the line.
How good it is,
a word spoken in the right season.
The who, what, why, and where depicts the reason.
Now, the season will give them the best platform for receiving
as it gives you the right platform for relieving.
That's why we are to never rush to judgment, but apply mercy
that can be found in God's glory.

Treating the occasion as if it was your story.
What would you have them to do?
Their ability to make a decision,
their ability to form an opinion,
must be discerned and evaluated,
not rushed through, but belated.
Then, at the end,
by God, how would you,
not them, be rated?

101

Every Way

He gave witty ideas
all through the years.
The very means for your prosperity,
purposed for you with clarity.
With that, what will you do?
Will you choose not to follow through?
Will you decide to hide it somewhere
because you do not care?

He knows you have the ability.
Why not lean on loyalty?
Will you choose not to follow through?
Why, unknown even to you?

When He returns, He will meddle.
His accounts, He will settle,
revealing how and why you failed.
Too much to do to follow through.
No funds to get started, so weak-hearted.
Expected rejection because of reflection.
No hope to receive what was believed.
I couldn't trust You to bring me through.

Believe you me,
you will not escape His scrutiny.
He said, "When I come back, will I find faith?"
Should a lie be the default you choose to use,
just the same,
He's ahead of your game
because He knows all things.
Wherever you are, He's there.
If you spoke it, He heard it.
Before you thought it, He saw it.
Think about it.
He was the One to say it:
"When I come back, will I find faith?"
Faith to do what He expects you to do.
When it lines up with the Word,
just do what you've heard.
When you don't,
to you, that's sin, you see,
given, you are under His authority.
He will say,
"My talent you buried in the ground.
"How sad for you.
"Your life could have been so much better.
"That was all I wanted to do:
"Increase you day by day,
"in every way.
"Health and wealth, to begin with.
"Not the doom and gloom you chose to end with.
"But health and wealth, to begin with.
"Not the sickness, pain, and shame
"because of no gain."

You seem to be digging your own grave,
with your own hand,
using a borrowed shovel,
at the devil's command.
Do you not know what to do?
This is the clue.
Always remember God will,
at all times, be ahead of you.
His thoughts are worlds beyond your view.
There is nothing in Him
to spark a thought of negativity,
should you have the ability, to examine the Trinity.
So, when it is in line with the Word,
do what you have heard.
For when you don't, that's sin, you see,
given you are under His authority.
Then He will say,
"My talent you buried in the ground.
"How sad for you.
"Your life could have been so much better.
"That was all I wanted to do.
"Increase you day by day,
"in every way."

Health, wealth, to begin with.
Not the doom and gloom you chose to end with,
but health and wealth to begin with.
Not the sickness, pain, and shame,
because of no gain.
All because you chose, not His reign.

102

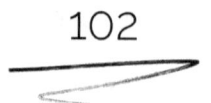

Credibility

Our God is credible,
not forgettable,
with love that's beyond measurable.
If you think you don't need to know Him,
you'd better think again, amen, amen.
You'd better think again, amen.

Oh, so credible, He is to be believed.
And if so, then,
why not receive?
He deserves your confidence.
No reason to recoil.
No reason to rescind.
We don't fall back or shrink in fear of Him.
Our reactions should always bring us near to Him.
Should we falter,
we'll return—return to this God of whom we learn.

Repudiation is never the action I take.
I never question His validity.
Him, I validate.
I declare, I mark with indication of official sanction.
It's there upon my heart.
From Him, I will never depart.

His Word contains the promises
from which the conclusion must be derived.
Not the thoughts from the so-called learned.
For we know how that was contrived.
Most often deducted from a premise,
the very strength of the backslide.
That's someone who often
has something in the heart to hide.
We don't fall back or shrink in fear of Him.
Our reaction should always bring us near to Him.
Should we falter, we'll return,
return to this God of whom we learn.

O, so credible, He is to be believed.
And if so, then why not receive?
He deserves your confidence.
No reason to recoil.
No reason to rescind.

103

At Last

Commit your ways to the Lord.
You can trust Him with that task.
He will bring it to pass,
at last, at last, at last.

He brought our righteousness to light.
Our judgments can shine so bright.
He will bring it to pass,
at last, at last, at last.

Trust in the Lord and do good,
while you dwell in the Lord, as you should.
More fed, more led
than in the past,
at last, at last, at last.

He brought our righteousness to light.
Our judgments can shine so bright.
He will bring it to pass,
at last, at last, at last.

When we delight ourselves in the Lord,
He gives the desires of our heart.
That's where we hide the Word.
Nothing there will we abort.

He brought our righteousness to light.
Our judgments can shine so bright.
He will bring it all to pass,
at last, at last, at last.

104

Thoughts

Because His thoughts are higher,
much broader and wider,
how can I have His thoughts,
and vote so very wrong,
considering, His thoughts on abortion,
are so very strong?
It doesn't take a rocket scientist to figure this out.
A heart filled with God knows what it is about.
Think just a moment on this notion,
with your heart settled in devotion.
That helpless unborn one is more than just matter.
Don't take those parts and just scatter.
For a selfish issue,
please don't destroy that baby's tissue.
That is a real child in the making.
What on earth are you thinking?
There is only one God who can create.
To follow through with this? What level of hate.
So, when the one with this degrading thought
on their platform,
runs for election,
for a Christian, this should be an easy selection.
Just stay on God's side.
There will be no reason to hide.
When you stay on God's side.
No sin or shame, in Jesus' name.

So, what if you overcome and really vote?
If the way you, do it,
our God, you provoke.
There in His sight,
you did it,
but you did it wrong.
What a negative heart throng.
It should not have been a difficult battle:
an innocent life against lying chatter.
However, you confused the matter,
and those parts did scatter.

No treaty here with peaceful relations,
when hate can be displayed throughout nations.

Copacetic

Back in the day,
we would say,
copacetic.
Should you use it today and not regret it,
some would think you quite pathetic.

It is not always known
where or why in society,
slang words are then shown.
For a length of time, they all ride that wave,
but before long, there goes that craze.
Words of the world are not always stable,
be they used in truth, fiction, or fable.
Words of the world are not always stable.

It is a wonder, you must admit,
how words of the Bible—
the B-I-B-L-E—
seem somehow to fit.
Within the society of Christianity,
not a word is ever lost.
Every word is heralded at all costs.
Nothing ever lost.

They are spoken during fellowship,
the outward activities of our relationship,
although broadly distinguished from other groups,
by doctrine and or creed.
The truth of the Son of God is what we need.
That binds us when it is believed.
It is amazing how that makes us to be
a God-perpetrating society.
Not with multiformity,
but with a godly variety.
It is the Word that forms us into who we now are,
from whom we were, by far.

Our last meeting with the Corpus Christi Christian Fellowship, with Pastor Leavell and Marva, was followed by an amazing happening. It was not even five days later, when we were traveling to our next place of ministry, that I noticed the billboard that is mentioned in the following rhyme. When I read the sign, it was a bit too early to connect it to anything relating to our previous visit with the Leavells, but immediately the Spirit of God began filling in the pieces. Pastor Leavell had spent a considerable amount of time sharing his experiences involving fasting. This composition was probably three-fourths complete before I could even make the connection. It would be good for you to hear his testimony in his own words.

Received from Pastor Leavell in text form on February 23, 2024:

> In response to my request for his testimony.
>
> This is a short version of what you asked for. On August 29, 2020, the Lord was impressing upon me to fast. I thought my fasting days were over because of the extensive fasting I had done previously. I was not sure that these seventy-seven days were of the Lord, because at the age of sixty, He seemed to be calling me to a forty-day fast, but I thought it was perhaps the enemy trying to kill me. I know that sounds strange. Nevertheless, I began a fast, not telling anyone outside my family. I was going to attempt to obey. Although Jesus had told me, I thought I might fail. However, I was able to finish that first forty-day fast, which was a miracle! Only God could do that!
>
> I would like to take you back briefly to 1981, when Jesus told me, through a dream, that I was to fast for forty-two days, three fourteen-day fasts. I woke up from the dream saying, "I cannot do that—it will kill me." Although I had fasted since the third grade—either one-, two-, or three-day fasts—I disobeyed the Lord for eight years. At that point, I was so embarrassed and hurt that I repented and promised God that I would obey Him even if it killed me. I began the first fourteen-day fast in September 1989. It was difficult, but I made it through. The second fast was in December of the same year, and in April 1990, I started the last of my three fourteen-day fasts. I had a dear friend who always fasted long fasts, and whom I knew would have wanted to know that I was going to a lake house to be alone with Jesus for fourteen days. I did not want any company, but out of respect for him, I told him what I was going to do. He insisted that he go with me. I really did not want him to come, and I tried to discourage him many, many times, but he refused to be dissuaded.
>
> I relented in my efforts to dissuade him and yielded to his insistence that he accompany me. It was during that time that, after praying many

hours a day, I asked him how old he was. He said he was thirty-four years old. The Holy Spirit then spoke to me that I was thirty-four years old when He had first instructed me that I was to fast for a total of forty-two days, three fourteens. I was, at that time, forty-two years old, the same number of days the Lord had wanted me to fast. Although I had been very insistent that my friend did not accompany me, it was of God. I had been in disobedience for eight years because of fear, and now the Lord had showed me His hand upon me. The Lord had wanted me to fast for a total of forty-two days. And now I was forty-two years old, fasting with a man whom I had never wanted to accompany me, only because I wanted to be with Jesus, but the man was the very age I was when God first spoke to me. Amazing! I had walked eight years in disobedience—and the difference between our ages was eight years.

I completed my second forty-day fast at the age of sixty-four, and my third at sixty-seven and a half years old, only consuming water and very small quantities of apple juice. Now, there were seventy weeks of fasting. On August 29, 2020, the Lord was impressing upon me to fast. I labored with that inner sense that the Lord wanted me to fast because of my extensive fasting history. I was seventy-three years old, and was probably too old to fast, although I knew Moses was much older than I was when he did it.

So, on August 29, after sensing the Lord wanting me to start a fast, I did not eat that evening, just in case it was the Lord. I had much discussion with Him about it. Well, during the night, I had one of the most intensive battles of spiritual warfare that I have ever had! I felt like a man who was in a boxing ring with twenty-one-year-old Mike Tyson! I could not get away from the beating I was receiving through self-condemnation and a sense of unworthiness. When I woke up on August 30, 2020, I felt I could not preach to my congregation, and I sat at the foot of my bed, praying to the Lord, telling Him I was not able to preach. I kept telling Him things like, "I'm sorry, Lord, please forgive me. I know that no one is truly worthy, but I feel like the worst of Your servants."

I said things like that repeatedly! Then, after one of my repentant comments, the Holy Spirit came upon me in such an awesome way that I shouted, "I want this, I want this, I want it for all of the members of our church!" The Lord had done a miracle! I felt the power of God in me as I had never felt before, and it was amazing! I preached that Sunday!

106

The Fast

Saw a roadside sign,
that became indelibly stamped in my mind.
I read,
and this is what it said:
"What do vegetarians eat when they cheat?"
It showed a picture of a platter of meat.
Immediately the thought rose up within my heart,
one that did not soon depart.
So, I followed through with the thought.

Most Christians I know are active at the table.
May I add that is not fable.
When consuming food daily,
with no interruption,
surely that kind of eating demands gumption.
Gumption?
Never, ever thought of using that word
to describe food consumption.
Yes, gumption.
Gumption sounds rude.
And in this context,
it is somewhat crude,
for its very display can be spirited,
shrewd, aggressive,
and extremely excessive.

Prior to learning the above,
I gave gumption to the one
climbing the corporate ladder.
But it is the one sitting at your table,
saying constantly,
"Pass the platter."
To try bringing in the thought
of a fast at that time
would then be seen as a great undermine.
It may even be voiced how that action is unjust,
and that should be embarrassing to us,
for the fast is a must.

The Bible speaks to the issue of the fast.
How long has it been in the past
that you last did a fast?
Is that the correct question to ask?
Great for the body and mind,
the areas the fast can certainly refine.
A spiritual increase will be achieved,
most likely noticed before the fast is relieved.
A level of sensitivity to our God,
the issue here is not at all odd.

It is time to contribute
words of encouragement to this cause.
So, what will a fast do for the body
that will be positive and hearty?
The first that comes to my mind,
It halts that selfish daily decline.
Should those thoughts be about you and yours only,
eventually you'll be left lonely,
when you should be centered on the needs of others,
knowing as for us God covers.

You may like this sound:
fasting provides the opportunity
for the body to slow down,
especially when coming off an eating frenzy.
The definition is "to have eaten plenty."
God made our vessel to cooperate.
Even with just a little effort from us,
it will regenerate.
Our organs have the chance to slow down and function
at each junction,
at the speed to which they were designed
by our all-knowing God who refines.
Just that alone can extend your life.
Why forgo using this God-given advice?

The fast.
Do it for your own good.
As you would,
all things that you should.
The fast.
Not a thing of the past.
Incorporate it into your now.
Your God receives it
as a voluntary bow.
The fast.
Not my will, Father,
but Your will be done,
in respect of Jesus, Your only Son.
The fast.
At last, my God, at last,
the fast.

107

Abler

If there is any aborting to do,
let it not be of that desire
that God did not give to you.
Remember,
the devil is the author
of the killing of the young,
barely after life has begun.
Even he knows you could be blessed
with that daughter or son.
Please, get on with that life.
Don't be caught up with that level of strife.

It will cause you to deeply grieve.
This, you can believe,
will most certainly hinder your God-given right to receive.

Now, should that despicable act be in your history,
it's now time to enjoy your victory.
If you have truly repented,
there is no mystery.

For there is no sin greater than any others.
Although you may not feel that way,
should you have your druthers.
But I give God the glory, it is not up to you.
For when you truly repented of the issue, then God was through.
Nothing else left to do.
And He's certainly not back there in your history.
No, He's here in your present and future, you see,
in the place where you can now operate.
Opposite of the past, which sucks life as it degenerates.
So, get out of that fetal position.
Embrace the godly condition.
Pray, praise, give,
the good now live.
Tap into the hope, the joy you employ.
Don't forgo what you know,
like grace and
faith to run this race.
It has all been made available;
to you, infailable.
Know that you alone are the caretaker,
the abler,
with the power, skill, means, and opportunity to do,
marked by intelligence, that's all you.
Now add knowledge and competence—
why would there ever be reluctance,
depicted by unwillingness, disinclination,
may I say, driven by an ungodly sensation.
Once again, it has all been made available to you,
with not even one thing to redo.
You alone are the caretaker, the abler.

108

Hunch

I recall having heard Christians say,
not often but occasionally, one would relay,
how they, at some time or another, "had a hunch."
In fact, as I ponder,
that has been voiced a bit, not a bunch.
It would most certainly have had to have been intuitive at best.
With no godly involvement, if honestly,
even they would confess.
That's relating to or arising from intuition.
The first two letters of that word, *I-N, IN,*
identifies from which it comes,
the position.
Although unseated from within you,
you cannot always say it is from a safe venue.
For if God is not the source of the power
behind that thought,
you ought to label it naught.
Always strive for substantial biblical presence
to base your belief on.

I call that reverence:
reverence for the Father,
reverence for the Son,
reverence for the Word
taught by the Holy One,
reverence for their decision
to stay and not go away,
reverence for every thought and decree
that rise in me
from either of the Three.

109

Possession

Ananias and Sapphira, his wife,
sold a possession,
but kept back part of the price,
giving an ungodly confession.
They colluded to only give a part.
We say, honestly, that was in their heart.
Bold and confident, they laid it at the apostles' feet,
unaware the Holy Ghost had revealed that deceit.

Peter said, "Ananias, Satan gave you this thought.
"Lying to the Holy Ghost,
"a sin you did wrought.
"Keeping back part of the price,
"that was yours to do.
"The problem was, you lied through and through.
"As long as you had it,
"was it not your own?
"You bought it,
"you worked it.
"All that was known.
"Every decision was in your power.
"We wish you had, how very sad,
"what goes down this hour.
"Why did you conceive this in your heart?
"Give only a part.
"You did not lie to men, but to the God of the universe.

"You will pay a penalty.
"You will suffer the curse."

He did, he did, he fell down.
He gave up the ghost
as he lay on the ground.

Then came his wife, Sapphira,
in three hours,
with nothing different to say.
Because of that,
Peter cut off the chat.
She went the same day.
You can't lie to the Holy Ghost and get away.
Even though you may live to see another day.
We don't have to relive that moment in time.
Just keep it simple, tell the truth,
that will keep you in line.
You can't lie to the Holy Ghost and get away.
Even though you may live to see another day,
nothing good will come,
should you attempt to tempt the Spirit of God.
He's in this dispensation
to do administration.

110

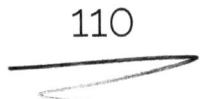

We Come

Full of riches is the great and wide sea,
where things are creeping innumerably.
There is that leviathan that You have made to play,
in the bright of the day.
So, we are in subjection unto You, Father of spirits and live,
for the peaceable fruit of righteousness You give,
through the voice of the Word,
which was heard.
So terrible was the sight that Moses said,
"I exceedingly fear and quake,"
but he endured for the people's sake.
Voicing how "they had come unto mount Zion,
"the city of the living God" from above.
We come to heavenly Jerusalem.
What a vast company of angels,
but we come to the Church,
where none of the above is unusual.
We come to the general assembly.
We come to the God and Judge of all,
who now protects us lest we fall.
We come to the spirit of just men made perfect.
There was a time when they just did not deserve it.
We come to Jesus, the Mediator of the new covenant.
He alone made our actions revenant.

We come to that blood of sprinkling for better things.
It speaks as it is released,
and great protection it brings.
We come to a Kingdom that cannot be moved.
Throughout perpetuity, that will be proved.
We come with reverence and godly fear,
to serve our God, who is acceptably here, so near.
We come.

111

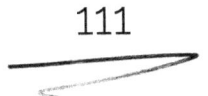

Forgive Me

Forgive me, God,
for having to hear You say it through someone else,
when I should have heard You for myself.
I don't want to give to You this day words through a song.
Just let me tell You straight out, O God, I was wrong.
Wrong in how I used Your hours of the day,
promising to get with You as time slipped away.
Wrong in clinging to my level of prayer,
when You wanted to take me deeper with care.
Wrong that not always when You beckoned me come,
did I always follow; other things got done.
Now I come.
I come, I come.
I drop down on my knees,
You to please.
Not to add another notch to my prayer gun,
not even assuring today it gets done.
Here I am, standing in need of prayer, for fellowship.
I'm not asking for one thing.
But an adoring desire I bring.
I come, I come.
The fact that I opened my eyes today
is amazing to me in every way.
That alone should make me want to stay.

Forgive me, Lord, for staying too long
where I didn't belong,
wasting time as if it were mine.
Every moment went by.
They all passed away.
Never did one moment stay.
Now I hear You say it for myself.
Now I respond to You,
no one else.

Not so long ago, referring to the previous words of poetry as "prayer,"
God made me to be aware.
This attachment goes out as an official announcement to the public,
so fitting is the nature of the subject.
Thank You, Lord, for correcting me:
A proclamation You will have it to be.
Not a prayer,
I now speak to all the readers out there.

Prayers go forth with restrictions.
We all should know.
A little of which you will read below.
Isaiah five and six,
listen to this:
"God will destroy those who speak leasing."
Well, what, may I ask, is "leasing"?
"Releasing"?
You may not know,
but engage me while I attempt to show,
the meaning of the word,
you just heard.

Replacement words could be
lies, falsehood, idolatry.
The main purpose for lying while praying,
to me, it seems,
would be to impress those who are hearing
what you are saying
while you are praying.
Now, when one is awed by their own words,
what comes next is an overwhelming urge,
and then comes the surge.
To repeat oneself is next on the rung,
simply because you like hearing you and no other one.
To you, no one is better than yourself.
No, not anyone else.
Not realizing you've degenerated your prayer to idolatrize.
Guard those words that they not become a compiled, defiled lie.
God hates that, believe you me.
Always lay a platform for victory,
as it should always be.

Perceive that first part not as a prayer,
but a statement of repentance that we are no longer there.
There, where?
Impotent in prayer,
that's where.
It matters not to me how you view this work.
Lyric, narrative, dramatic, whether told by someone else, or me,
rhythm or rhyme, you see.
Just perceive it not as a prayer.
I heard the word "proclamation."
To me, that was a revelation.

Should you need to,
then please do, too.
Do remember this:
We must all hear Him for ourselves,
that we may respond to Him and no one else.
Many have requested a copy of what I called a prayer.
Although I have in the past responded,
I can no longer go there.
Be anxious for nothing,
but in everything by prayer and supplication,
with thanksgiving,
let your request be made known to God,
for confirmation of this proclamation.

112

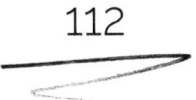

Aging

Aging is a process most shun
three or four decades after life has begun.
But this process we all must go through.
So, what is the alternative for you?
Think about this carefully.
Are you ready to rush to eternity?

Now, I am a Christian, and you may be, too.
If that statement is true,
it is, promised to us,
to those who place trust,
in the Holy One,
by so simply embarrassing His Son.
So that our future on the other side of time,
as we know it,
will be incessantly fluid—
as a continuum with no resistance,
pleasantly enrolled in forever existence.

Every new year of my life
comes with new insight.
I now perceive aging to be
not a push from this side,
with a slippery, rough ride.
I see it more to be,
for you and me,
that gentle, almost unrecognizable tug
of a weightless object.

During the process of a gradual lug,
not a drag,
nor a pull,
never a jerk, be aware,
but an unrecognizable, continual replacing,
from here to there,
with the deepest love and care.
It's a haul of a different kind,
administered by that loving God of all time,
not laboriously through strife,
but adventurously through life
while continuing to undertake
new and daring enterprises.
As another day arises,
the moving toward
that which is to be attained
continues to remain.
And through days, weeks, months,
years, and/or decades,
we will all arrive safe
to look upon the face
of the One
who so lovingly guided us
with care and trust.
This, of course, comes after that momentary blink.
That last action at the end of the link.
The beginning of a new way and day
that will afford us to never, ever be belated,
nor possible to be separated
from anyone who ever embraced
God's Son,
the everlasting Holy One.

113

Holy Matrimony

Holy matrimony!
One man, one woman—
all outside that is phony.
Spoken by the Creator of all that we see,
whomever we may be.
You did not make you—try arguing that
with a solid fact.

When your very Maker
deems your actions, desires, reflections to offend,
turn around, come back from where you are, do not contrive to bend.
Then, that's when
you will have displayed actions of reluctance.
Allow the Word to be your consultant.
Then you can truly understand
the power of your voice,
together with your choice,
engaging in true repentance,
with no damning acts of remembrance.
But should that lie try to invade your mind,
reflect on it with first John one and nine.
If we confess our sin,
He is faithful and He is just
to forgive us,
and cleanse from that unrighteous act.
That is the fact.

Holy matrimony,
one man, one woman—
all outside that is phony.
Spoken by the Creator of all that we see,
whomever we may be.
You did not make you.
That statement is true.
Try arguing that
with a natural fact.
You won't win.
It will be sin,
from the beginning
to the very end.

114

Prosperity

I am spending my days in prosperity,
my years in pleasure, too,
as I obey and serve You.

When calamity comes suddenly,
there will always be a remedy.
The feeling of anxiety
will not get a hold on me.
Attentively, I hear Your voice.
There is no other overriding choice.

The sound that goes out
of Your mouth—
where I go it will lead.
When I sleep, it will feed.
When I awake,
it will communicate.
Your commandment is a lamp,
Your law a light.
Reproof and instruction are the way of life.

115

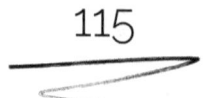

My Place in Battle

I will take my place in the battle.
I will keep my place in You, Lord.
I will not break rank
for there is no metal of thanks
when I break rank,
as the battle belongs to You, Lord.
You made what I now see.
You gave it to me.
I will give You due respect.
Nothing of Yours do I reject.
You made it,
then You gave it.
We lost it,
so You brought it back.
None can argue.
That's a given fact.

You know the one who stole it
will come for it again, again, and again.
So, You, Father, left not the plan
in the hand
of no other
outside of the Son of Man.

116

Tirhza

*W*hile pondering
thoughts of our heart,
it would be too difficult
to not impart
the disposition or our attitude,
as we are minded of you.

From day one,
a daughter, not a son.
Though not disappointed,
believing, too,
that day would surely come.
Cute as all get-out
you have always been.
As you got older, that did not end.
But much more important
than your appearance,
you had a way to always cheer us.
But how about when you disappeared once?
Because you wanted to steer us.

All those life issues we would most surely repeat.
In none of that was there ever defeat.
You cared for yourself, for the most part.
We should have known at adulthood that would not depart.
Independent as you could be,
we noticed at age three.
And why not, when self-sufficient at age two?
You pretty much, in most cases, knew what to do,
taking the leads always from your dad.
I will admit, prior to Christ,
sometimes it made me quite mad.
If he did it and you knew,
before the day was done,
you'd have another notch on your gun.
To you, he could do no wrong.
That, in itself,
made your persistence strong.
That was the force that caused you to be
independently self-sufficient and worthy,
to have a wonderful family of your own.

—Mommy

117

Great Grace

We have been with Jesus.
And that you know.
For that boldness
in us did show.
A notable miracle has been done.
Glory and honor to God's Son.
Spreading ahead among the people,
threats of censoring—how evil.
God's Son, you cannot deny—don't even try.
To command us not to speak is weak,
demanding we do not teach in Jesus' name—
how freak.
His character, His purpose, we must expose,
how He died and how He rose.
It is not right in God's sight to hearken to you,
day or night.
We cannot but speak His name.
The things that we have seen and heard,
we proclaim.
His name is Jesus.
Jesus, my Lord, the mighty King,
my Master and the reason I sing.
All who see and glorify God
will, in the future, have their reward.
When a miracle is done through the Son,
great grace is upon each one.
Great grace upon you.
Great grace upon you, too.
Great grace upon you, and you, and you.

118

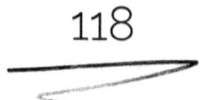

Ya Gotta Wanna

You may be broken up into more pieces
than can be gathered by a rake.
It's time to put it altogether again,
for the Kingdom's sake.
Don't shy away
and hide all day
in the nearest corner.
Have a heart check.
Get a stiff neck.
But ya gotta wanna.
Ya gotta wanna use all awarded
by our Lord and Savior.
We can use that to check that unruly behavior,
but ya gotta wanna use all awarded
by our Lord and Savior.

119

I Am

"*I* am that I am,"
is what He said.
"That is who I am.
"Not ever will My name change.
"It will never cease to be."

"I am that I am."
He said that to me.
"That is who I am.
"My name will always remain the same,
"forever and ever,
"My name will be.
"What is your need?
"I am THAT,
"I am.
"Whatever the need,
"I am the seed.
"I am that I am."

Ponder that thought in your heart.
"My very name will impart.
"And this is My memorial
"unto all generations,
"north, south, east, west of all nations."

Your thought for today,
I now say:
"Evil spirits will not leap on you,
"overcome you,
"prevail against you.
"You will not be the one to run
"because you will have the victory
"before the battle is begun."

120

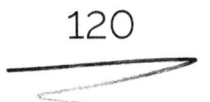

Perspective

Are you of the thought
that you can lose your part?
There is leading in the Word,
I believe.
But as for me,
once saved, always saved.
How powerful His blood
that He gave.
There will be no sedition
in my condition.
I'll not uprise,
nor organize opposition,
as in rebellion, defiance, in cahoots
with the dueling majority,
nor overthrow,
go against all I know,
about the ruling authority.
I am not reticent about telling you the truth
I've no reason to.
No, I won't leave.
I will just hold on tight and cleave.
I continue to persist
in what I believe.
That is where I exist.
I believe I'll just hold on tight and cleave.

Won't leave,
just cleave.
You cannot pull me away
because I want to stay.
You can knock me down,
but I'll stick around
because I'm cleaving.
Not leaving, cleaving.
I persist
to continue and exist.
Exist in what I believe,
all centered around the cleave.
What is your elective
on this perspective?

121

Oh, Magnify the Lord with Me

The angel of the Lord encamps them
that fear Him,
and delivers them.
Oh, magnify the Lord with me.
I sought the Lord.
He heard my prayer,
delivered me from all my care.
Oh, magnify the Lord with me.
Oh, taste and see that the Lord is good.
Blessed is the one who trusts Him as he should.
Oh, magnify the Lord with me.
Oh, fear the Lord, you,
His saint.
There will always be want to them who are faint.
Oh, magnify the Lord with me.
You don't have to lack and suffer hunger.
Just seek the Lord
and want no longer.
Oh, magnify the Lord with me.
I depart from evil,
good I do.
Peace pursues, too.
Oh, magnify the Lord with me.

The eyes of the Lord are upon me.
His ears are opened unto me.
I cry, and the Lord hears me
and delivers me
out of tears,
because He hears.
Oh, magnify the Lord with me.

122

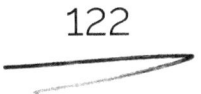

Here's a Reverberating Sound

Here's a reverberating sound.
I'm not lost.
I was found.
When Jesus came in,
He forgave all my sin.
That's where my old life did end.
From the topsoil of earth, we did rise.
Not worth much then,
but God knew when
we would be His greatest prize.
He wanted for a place to reside,
in the heart of the one He'd provide
from a piece of the ground.
Just look around.
We were the greatest of all.
Lost, but now found.
Here's a reverberating sound.
I'm not lost;
I was found, when Jesus came in,
forgave all my sin.
That's when my old life did end.

Planting into rich soil
will not eliminate toil.
We strive to stir up.
We labor continuously,
advancing maybe.
Not without difficulty,
but in the end,
we win.

The goal is to produce fruit much like Him.
Early on,
that may seem dim.
He came in and planted His love from above.
The root of all things good.
Nothing left out,
without a doubt.

The way He would do it, we should.
Emphatically, we could.

Here's a reverberating sound.
I'm not lost,
I was found.
When Jesus came in,
forgave all my sin,
that's when my old life did end.

The ark was overlaid with pure gold.
A crown of gold,
I'm told.
Gold even overlaid the wood,
as most certainly it should.
That tabernacle
served its purpose
throughout that preservice,
satisfying God and man,
for that was most surely the plan.
But the future would offer the best endeavor,
for where God would settle forever,
was in you and me, if in Jesus we are free
to return to that old life never.

Gold in our world is costly,
but it provides no reproductive ability.
How many trace minerals for life's existence are there in our soil?
And oh, how working with it and through it we do toil.
Yes, that gave us the start for that future,
godly impart,
of His occupation of the heart.

123

You Mold Our Hearts

Lord, You look from heaven and behold
from the place of Your habitation.
All the sons of men, You see.
All the peoples of the nation.

To help man,
You press where needs be.
Through the squeezing into shape,
that's what You did for me.
 Molding into form,
to help one to relate,
a determined resolution,
that desired conclusion.
Oh! You fashion our hearts alike
in conjunction with all our works of plight.

Your eye is upon those who fear You.
Mercy is not only what You do.
Mercy is a major part of You.
As love is not a commodity
you own; love is who you are,
what you are,
all that you are, by far.
Through mercy and love,
You mold our hearts.
How can I from You ever depart?
You mold my heart.

124

Come with Thanksgiving

I come with thanksgiving into Your presence,
bringing psalms,
a form of joyful noise,
as I am poised.

O Lord,
O my great God,
O my great King,
Your praise,
Your worship, I bring.
The sea is Yours because You made it.
The dry ground also belongs to You.
You formed at the right time.
None was belated.
The deep places of the earth
are eternal evidence of Your worth.
The strength of the hill,
because of You, stands still.
So, I come with thanksgiving in Your presence,
with much evidence.
I bow to worship You,
for this is what I desire to do.

Kneeling before You, Lord, my Maker, in respect of You.
I'm not totally centered on what You do.
I am more centered on You,
just You.
For You are our God,
and we are Your people.
Because You want to be our God,
and we want to be Your people.
So, we come, we come.
I come.

The Greatest Sound I've Ever Heard

Thank You, Lord, for Your Word,
the greatest sound I've ever heard.
It always helps me through my day,
even when I think I know the way.
It shows me clearly what to do,
like this or that;
go here, go there.
Stop!
Don't go anywhere.
Then and only then can I settle down and listen.
Thank You, Lord, for Your Word, the greatest array of my day.
It's better than the finest meal,
a once-in-a-lifetime deal,
always delicious,
satisfying, and sufficient.
Well, here I go again,
running that process through on demand.
There it was, that same Word directing me.
There was no new word, you see,
showing me clearly what to do,
like this or that;
go here, go there.
Stop!
Don't go anywhere.
This word is the Word
that I have already heard.

So I quiet myself to understand,
be it a statement or request or demand.
There's no other way to begin my day,
but to obey.
I never want to slight the Spirit.
Whatever the answer to my need,
how would I hear it?
So, I hanker unto my Teacher, my Friend so dear
and submit to what I hear.
Well, here I go again,
running that process through on demand.
When I finally settle down and listen,
I'm doing this.
I'm doing that.
I'm going here.
I'm going there.
I stop.
I don't go anywhere.
There I hear once again the Word,
but there was no new word directing me,
but that same Word I'd already heard,
again, and again and again.
It continued until I gave in.
The Spirit was not the one needing a change,
nor was I the one
needing to remain.
So, quieting myself to understand,
be it a statement or request on demand,
it is key—that's the key
so vital for every victory.
There's no other way
to begin my day
than to obey
the command without delay.

While our son Cris was visiting with us some time last year, he said, "Mom, I want to visit the catacombs." I had absolutely no idea what led up to that, and I was somewhat surprised he had voiced that desire. A few days later, Marcel and I left for our weekly ministry trip. Well, lo and behold, I turned the radio on, and there was a program playing about the catacombs. God started talking to me in that moment, and I hope you are blessed by His thoughts.

126

Catacombs

Ezekiel, Ezekiel,
your testimony not at all surreal.
No depersonalization-derealization disorder
to feel.
For it is not bizarre.
It is the Word of God on par—
not mixed with fiction and fantasy,
but the truth in all reality.
Upon you rested your God's hand.
It was He who carried you out,
and that, you clearly understand.
He set you down amid the valley
 of dry bones.
Let's just call it the catacombs.
Those bones were dry.
No one wondered why.
It had been a long time since
those physical structures were alive.
And presently they're still un-revived.

God said to you, "Ezekiel, can
"these bones live,
"son of man?"
Well, all of humanity
would have agreed with you
that only our God knew that was true.
So, He said to prophesy unto those bones.
We know now a miracle would be shown.
But to think that which ends up in the catacombs
is the end of one's biological structure
is so very wrong.
That thought had lingered far too long.
Because of the Word of God,
depressing ideas concerning the catacombs
can soon be gone.
I endeavor to never forever surmise
that my bones won't live again.
What about you?
Can I hear an amen!?!
Amen, amen!

The End

Prayer

Now the God of peace that brought you again from the dead,
our Lord Jesus, that great Shepherd of the sheep,
through the blood of the everlasting covenant,
make you perfect in every work, to do His will,
working in you that which is well pleasing in His sight,
through Jesus Christ, to whom be glory forever and ever.
AMEN!

Hebrews 13:20

ABOUT THE AUTHOR

Evelyn Joseph founded Sword and Psalm Ministry in 1984 alongside husband, Marcel Joseph, Jr. The two have traveled extensively across the United States and internationally to teach the Word. Evelyn fulfills the occupation of a teacher within the five-fold ministry, bringing clarity and insight to believers worldwide.

You may contact Evelyn at

eajmj@yahoo.com

Box 471023

Tulsa, OK 74147